# Edward Wolfe

John Russell Taylor

# Edward Wolfe

Trefoil Books,
for Odette Gilbert Gallery, London

Produced by Trefoil Books Ltd., 7 Royal Parade, Dawes Road, London SW6



Set in Ehrhardt by Suripace Limited, Milton Keynes
Printed by BAS Printers, Over Wallop.

# I

To those who knew Edward Wolfe only towards the end of his long life, it must have seemed he could never have been much different. Old age in many respects became him – not because he took on naturally the mantle of the Grand Old Man, but precisely because he did not. Even belatedly received into the Establishment – he was not made a Royal Academician until he was 75 – he always retained a quality of the outsider-by-choice. Diminutive in stature, twinklingly mischievous in manner, he suggested some kind of ageless elfin presence, everybody's slightly disreputable uncle, carrying with him a hint of bohemia into even the most strait-laced gatherings.

During his lifetime, it was difficult to tell just how far these impressions were justified, and just how closely they related to his art. Voluble on all manner of subjects, and infinitely interested in the world about him, Teddy Wolfe was oddly reticent about himself. He could, indeed, be maddeningly evasive about the details of his own history, as several eager researchers discovered. Where his art was concerned, he projected a curious mixture of confidence and unconcern. He welcomed the measure of official recognition which came to him eventually, but felt, it seems, that it came too late – after, certainly, the vital part of his creative work was done.

His reservations on this score do not appear to have arisen from natural modesty: he had at least his fair share of the artist's egotism and belief in his own ultimate importance. But he felt that he had been kept beyond the pale through the personal enmity of a handful of powerful people, and his naturally feckless life-style, careless of his artistic progeny once he had done with them, as unconcerned with money when he did not have it (which was frequently) as when he did, did not exactly contribute to his readily receiving the regard of those who measured success by conventional standards. To the end he was sublimely unrespectable.

All this meant that, even as an RA, Wolfe remained something of an outsider. His spirit was certainly profoundly non-conformist, whatever standard it might be expected to conform to. Not that he was in all respects unworldly. He enjoyed society, even with a capital 'S', and had many friends and patrons among the rich and famous, though he always liked them for what they were rather than who they were, and could never be persuaded reliably to play the Establishment game: the tradition of early twentieth-century artistic bohemianism was too deeply embedded in his own nature, and for that matter in his eccentric background.

By the end of his life his art had ceased to challenge or outrage, as its generally Post-Impressionist vocabulary had come to be accepted into the language of the tribe: in that respect at least he was reasonably at home in the Royal Academy of the 1970s. But throughout his active career it had remained constantly challenging in the deeper sense – the only sense that counts: like all genuine and sometimes great art, it was finely unpredictable, carried this way and that by the tides of inspiration, and finally, for all its immediate sensuous appeal, sublimely unconcerned with whether it pleased or not. Wolfe

2

always followed a different drummer. That made him difficult to pin down, pigeonhole and assess during his lifetime. But retrospectively it is the clearest guarantee we could wish of his status as a modern master.

## II

Edward Wolfe was born in Johannesburg on May 29 1897. Astrologers might find the date of his birth significant: by Western standards he grew up to be a typical Gemini, charming and mercurial, and by Eastern a very credible product of the year of the Rooster, witty, attractive, abrasive and eccentric. The significance of the place of birth is more arguable. Its exoticism attracted attention when he was first working in England: Roger Fry labelled him rather fancifully 'a little African savage with a genius for lampshades'. But it is quite likely that his subjection to the sights and colours of Africa early in his life had more than a little to do with his later passionate response to colour and warmth around him, and his need constantly to re-create them if they did not exist.

His family background was by any standards peculiar. His father Eli Wolfe was a Lithuanian Jew, his mother Ruth Elizabeth Wedderburn a Presbyterian from the Scottish border. Quite how they met and married does not seem to be recorded: Eli had left Lithuania in the 1870s in search of fortune, if not necessarily fame, and was quite a noted figure in South Africa by the time of Edward's birth. Known for some reason as 'Chinaman Wolfe', he was a famous gambler and investor, much given to flamboyant gestures like lighting his cigars with five-dollar bills. He was hardly the most reliable of heads for the family – Edward remained an only child – and there seem to have been violent arguments between the parents long before Eli met his somewhat mysterious death in 1905, falling (perhaps pushed) off the balcony of a gambling house. At any rate, he left the world penniless, and Ruth had instantly to set to and keep herself and young Edward by the labours of her needle.

The stereotypical image of Edward's mother that this suggests would be that of the tight-lipped puritan, bearing bitterly with her husband's profligacy and bringing up her son to fear some fierce Presbyterian God. Perhaps fortunately, the truth does not measure up to this convenient fantasy. Ruth Elizabeth Wolfe was clearly a formidable lady, but by no means as unworldly as one might suppose. In her early years she had been involved in show business and travelled extensively before coming to rest in South Africa. An uncle had achieved moderate fame and fortune on the halls with an animal act billed as 'Leoni Clark, The Cat King', and Ruth herself played stage mother to her younger sisters when they had an act which toured the halls all over America. Certainly her ideas of religion were open enough for her to send Edward, when he was old enough for schooling, to the Marist Brothers Catholic school in Johannesburg.

Her own history also made her remarkably receptive to the possibilities open to an artistically-inclined son. Not that she seems ever to have had any specific artistic ambitions for him, but such as he developed during his childhood and youth she was perfectly happy to go along with. Virtually from the beginning young Edward seems to have been a chirpy, extrovert child, happy in the limelight, basking in the attention of others, and ever ready to perform. The only thing left for long undefined was the ultimate form the performance might take. Would it be literal performance on the stage? Would it be something musical, for very soon Edward gave signs of more-than-serviceable musical talents? Or might he, after all, make something of the talent for drawing which soon impressed, and no doubt seemed most respectable in its prospects to, the Marist Brothers?

Before this could become in any way a practical issue, however, Edward made the first long journey in a life which was to contain much travel. After the death of his father, his mother resolved on a return to England as soon as it was financially possible. There seemed to be no spare money anywhere in the family, and even if there had been, out in South Africa there was little prospect of laying hands on it, so Ruth, not for the first or the last time in her life, set about repairing the family fortunes herself. A woman of many and various gifts, and even more importantly of tremendous determination, she became a busy and quite successful dressmaker, and in two years had put aside enough money to take her and Edward to London.

They were not to see the capital from a very advantageous position: they could afford to take only modest rooms in Bethnel Green, and the thing which most impressed itself on the ten-year-old Edward's memory was the presence of a music-hall just opposite, where such famous or soon-to-be famous names as Marie Lloyd and Charlie Chaplin could be seen performing: indeed it was here in 1907 that Charlie Chaplin had the major disaster

3

4

5

of his life as a comic when an ill-conceived solo act as a Jewish comedian (this was several years before the immortal tramp persona) was booed off the stage its very first night. It is unlikely that young Edward was present on that unfortunate occasion, but at least his mother, child of show business herself, had no rooted objection to his seeing live theatre, not always of the most reputable sort, at first hand.

Though Mrs Wolfe did not, in her own estimation, achieve very much during the two years she and Edward spent in London, she did at least make enough money to return to South Africa in modest style, with a nest-egg of £500, which was then a considerable amount. Unfortunately she had an excessively trusting side to her nature, and on the boat back let herself be sweet-talked by a plausible-seeming couple into entrusting her savings to them – with which, on arrival at the Cape, they promptly vanished, leaving the Wolfes completely without resources again. But Ruth was not one to be nonplussed by this turn of events: she made straight for the most expensive hotel in town, frankly explained the position, and asked if it was all right to stay on credit until she got straight again. Impressed – or perhaps merely taken unawares by her sheer cheek – the manager agreed, and that was precisely what happened.

No doubt with such a mother it was not surprising that young Edward should evince a precocious histrionic talent. And Ruth was perfectly willing, and with her early experience able, to back it. So began Edward's first career, as a child star of the South African stage. 'Star' is perhaps slightly overstating the case, but with his mother's encouragement he managed to attract the attention of two notable actor-managers in South Africa, joined first Charles Howett's company then Leonard Rayne's, and between the ages of thirteen and sixteen he played most of the major child roles of the current repertoire in the main urban centres and on tour – aided by his smallness and slightness of stature, which enabled him to get away with playing roles far younger than his actual years.

The only drawback to this precocious career was that it meant his formal schooling in effect ended when he was ten, and though in later life he was extremely articulate and well-informed, he always felt disadvantaged by his paucity of structured education. It was to make up in some degree for this lack that in 1914, at seventeen, voice broken and beard sprouting, at last decisively too old to play children any more, he decided to give up the stage, settle in Johannesburg and go to night school, keeping himself by working during the day in a jeweller's shop. He was still not too clear what he wanted to do with his life. Acting seemed quite easy and it was what he was most experienced in. But other possibilities were opening up too – especially after he met one of the most influential people in his young life, a young pianist and music teacher from New Zealand called Barclay Donne.

Dodie, as Edward called him, was clearly a charismatic figure, at any rate in the context of artistic Johannesburg. He was much impressed by Edward's potential, and was the first member of either sex to fall under the spell of his potent, unpredictable charm. He undertook to tutor Edward in music – always to remain a major interest and influence in his adult life – and also recognised a more than average talent in his early attempts at drawing and painting; to such an extent that he encouraged Edward to think of painting as a conceivable profession and arranged for the British painter George Smithard to give him lessons. The teacher-pupil relationship rapidly became something more intense, and soon Edward and Dodie were living together, sharing everything.

It was Dodie's notion that he and Edward needed the wider artistic horizons of London to expand their respective talents, and he persuaded Edward's mother to let him take Edward to England. They arrived in 1916, and set up house together in Maida Vale. Though Britain was at war, and many young artists had gone to the Front, some of them, like Henri Gaudier-Brzeska and Isaac Rosenberg, never to return, Edward was not considered strong enough to be required for military service. His ambitions were still not too precisely defined, but all ways seemed open to him: he immediately won scholarships, both of which he took up, to the Regent Street Polytechnic to study art and to the D'Aurban School of Dramatic Art, where he hoped to extend and deepen his skills as an actor. At school, Frank Benson saw him act and was sufficiently impressed to offer him the role of St Francis in a provincial tour. But the longer he stayed in London, the more centrally interested he found himself in painting, and the more involved he became with London art life, so he refused and determined to concentrate all his efforts on art instead.

Barclay Donne naturally also had his ambitions, but these met with less success. He is reported to have been a fine but excessively temperamental concert pianist, inclined to develop something like paranoia when things did not work out quite as he hoped. He managed, as well as teaching, to get some concert engagements, but there was a major drama when he muffed his big chance because, he alleged, his 'enemies' gave him drink in the interval so that he made a hash of the concerto in the second half and could never play in public again. Whatever the rights and wrongs of that particular story, there seems no doubt that while Edward's star ascended Dodie's stayed dispiritingly just where it was. Edward soon got to know everybody, and, being gregarious and outgoing, was invited everywhere. The gloomy and introspective Dodie stayed at home in Maida Vale and brooded, and of course got very bitter and jealous, darkly suspecting Edward of infidelities which in fact he never committed, remaining strictly faithful to Dodie and parrying all other propositions, whomever from, throughout their five-year association. The affair lasted, in increasingly difficult circumstances, until 1919, when Edward was compelled for reasons of health to return to South Africa and Dodie vanished from London also – it is thought to his native New Zealand.

Before that happened, however, Edward's life had been totally transformed. He had been launched as a professional, and widely admired, artist, he had become one of the Bloomsbury Group, and had learnt to mingle with unconcerned delight among the intellectual and artistic elite of the day. And this had all happened with dazzling suddenness. In 1917 he decided to give up his acting ambitions altogether and concentrate entirely on painting – to which end he left the Poly and the drama school and enrolled instead at the Slade, then one of the three most prestigious art schools in the country and certainly the most progressive. Under the tutelage particularly of Henry

6

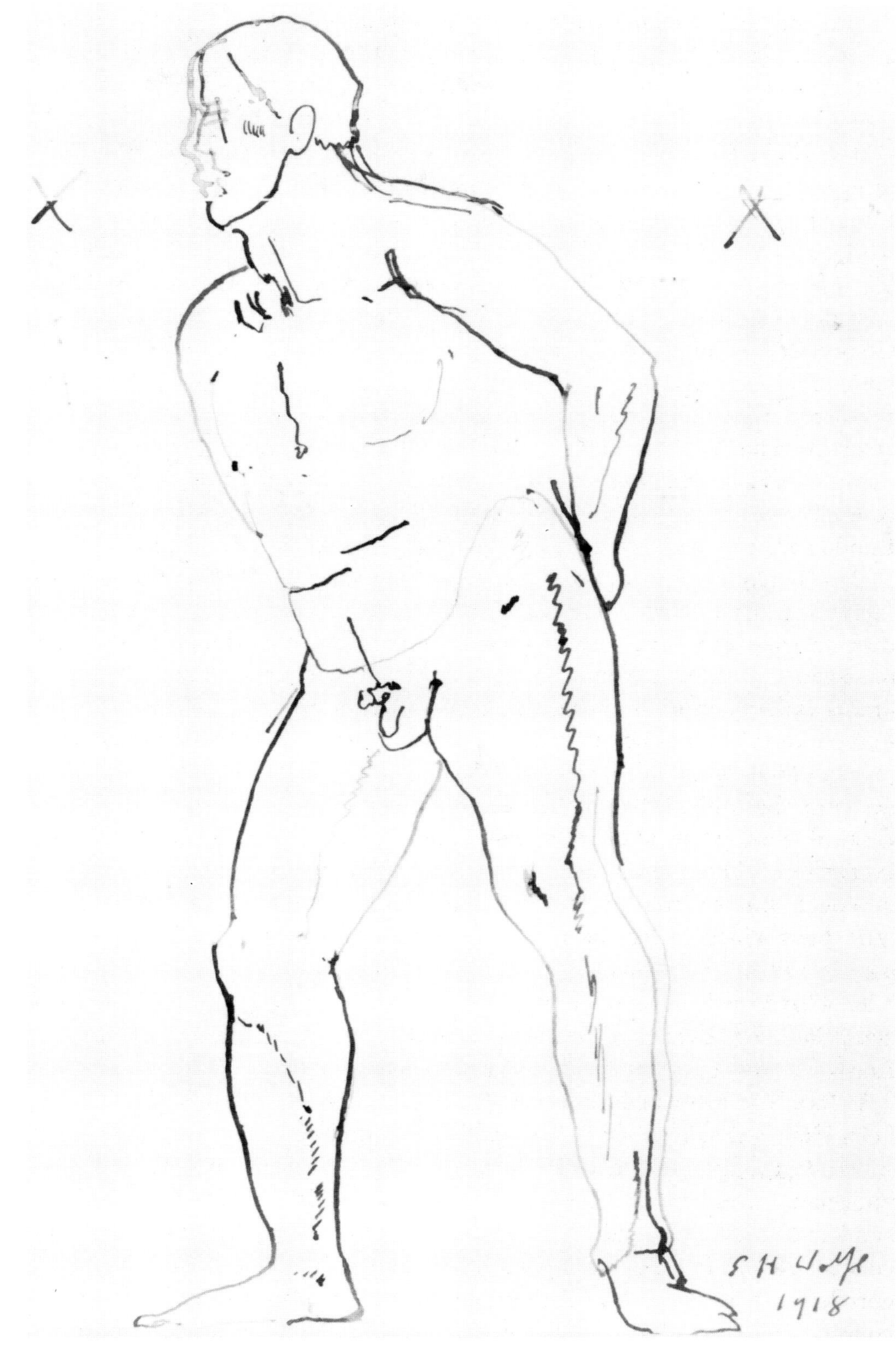

7

Tonks, the school had gone through one of its greatest periods immediately before the First World War, with an amazing line-up of soon-to-be-notable students, including Gertler, Bomberg, Meninsky, Wadsworth, the Spencers (Stanley and Gilbert), Paul Nash, Matthew Smith, Vanessa Bell, Duncan Grant, Dora Carrington, Alvaro Guevara, C.R.W. Nevinson, William Roberts and Ben Nicholson.

When Edward joined the Slade it happened, quite by chance, that a generation of distinguished future theatre designers were in immediate prospect, including Rex Whistler, Oliver Messel and Roger Furse. But for the moment there was something of a lull while many of the most promising young men were off at the Front. There was, however, at least one young woman around whom it was difficult not to notice: the irrepressible Nina Hamnett, later more famous as a rioter and reveller, uninhibited autobiographer (*Laughing Torso*; *Is She a Lady?*) and fixture of London's artistic bohemia around Fitzroy Street than as, strictly speaking, an artist. But in 1917 she was still young and enterprising and ready to work as hard at her art as at her social and sexual life. With this in mind she had drifted into the orbit of Bloomsbury, and knew Roger Fry, the great arbiter of visual taste for the group, influential critic and organizer of the Omega Workshop, a rather gentlemanly (or ladylike) institution dedicated to carrying the message of modern art to the affluent but generally conservative middle classes by way of enterprising interior design and decoration.

Edward got to know Nina Hamnett – meeting her first at a party given by Augustus John –, and through her Roger Fry. Fry was always looking for new artistic recruits to lend a hand with the more menial work of the Omega Workshops. Not that anything which served the cause of modern art and good taste was regarded as menial, you understand, but it cannot be pretended either that the anonymous production of, for example, handpainted paper or parchment candle-shades, all to an established formula, was necessarily the most stimulating and enlivening task an ambitious young artist might be set. That, precisely, was the first job Edward was tried out on, and he acquitted himself superbly, introducing sprightly variations into the abstract designs he was given as a model and turning out what was required with speed and fluency as well as a lively invention. 'Ah, yes, Wolfe – a perfect genius for candle-shades,' Fry observed to Duncan Grant, already a member in good standing and a painter to watch. Before long Edward was promoted to more responsible jobs, designing and painting trays and decorating furniture.

In the winter of 1917-18 he also got his first direct taste of the London theatre, when he assisted Fry in the design and making of sets and costumes for the first act of *Too Much Money*, a play by Israel Zangwill which went on with Lillah MacCarthy at the Ambassadors Theatre. Unfortunately, not one piece of Omega craft certainly attributable to Edward seems to survive, though we can no doubt guess at their style from the generality of anonymous examples, and from some evidently rather similar pieces Edward produced by himself in the early Twenties. And there is one other important piece of evidence, in the shape of a *Still Life with Omega Cat*, once Duncan Grant's and now belonging to the Charleston Trust, which is Edward's first surviving datable painting, crisply inscribed on the back 'my first study/painted in 1918 Edward Wolfe/in Nina Hamnett's studio/Fitzroy St.' Along with a glass container and a bunch of bananas it depicts unmistakably an Omega jug (chipped), a small ceramic figure of a cat produced for the Omega Workshops by Henri Gaudier-Brzeska and the richly patterned jacket of an Omega Workshops publication. And the style is even more interesting to observe: with its vibrant colour and its excitedly tilted, crowded composition, it clearly reflects a view of art which must come directly from the influence of Roger Fry.

Much has been made – too much, probably – of Tonks's rooted opposition to Fry, Post-Impressionism and all that they stood for. It seems certain that what Tonks and his followers at the Slade objected to was not so much the actual art of the Post-Impressionists, introduced to Britain by Fry in two very influential exhibitions, 1910 and 1912, as to the idea of movements in taste being 'promoted' by critics and commercial interests. But it is unlikely Edward would have imbibed from his teachers at the Slade any encouragement to emulate the leading lights among the French Post-Impressionists exhibited by Fry, particularly Matisse, who had dominated the second Post-Impressionist show and was to remain a profound influence throughout Edward Wolfe's life. With a bit of hindsight we can already see a hint of Matisse in the *Still-Life's* range of colour, though at this early stage in Edward's development the evidence of Cézanne in the composition is perhaps more immediately evident. Whichever, the powerful and immediate effect of Roger Fry's tastes on the young painter can hardly be mistaken.

Contact with Fry and the Omega Workshops did not only open the door for him to Post-Impressionism and all that implied in bolder colour and the free handling of form. It also introduced him, by an unexpected route, to abstraction. Though in easel painting the abstract was still considered very avant-garde and beyond the comprehension not only of the public at large, but even of the most expert practitioners of the arts themselves – Ben Nicholson, for instance, who was to be the most famous British abstractionist of the interwar years, hardly ventured on completely non-figurative work until the end of the Twenties. But there was a loophole. Those first painted candle-shades Edward produced for Fry were decorated with abstract designs, and so was much of Omega's more practical product. Of course: that was what buyers expected, even from far more traditional pieces, because it was overtly decoration, not meant to be isolated from the function of the piece and looked at in itself. You did not ask what a jug or a tray or a lampshade *meant*; but you might well ask that of a self-sufficient painting in a frame on a wall.

Nevertheless, the possibilities of pure form, without representational connotations, did come to fascinate Edward, and he began a series of abstract drawings and paintings which was to continue throughout his working life. Many of them, admittedly, were or might have been intended to garnish Omega objects, or similar things that he went on producing on his own account long after the demise of Omega itself. But still the idea and the interest are there, if perhaps a little shame-facedly pursued. Bryan Robertson, in his introduction to the catalogue of the 1967 Wolfe retrospective, describes Edward in the Sixties producing abstracts from the recesses of his studio rather in 'the way in which an entirely happily married pillar of respectability might suddenly confide to you a dazzling series of photographs of *louche* mistresses.'

If abstraction was the louche mistress in relation to the representational art to which Edward was always wedded, she was at least well looked after, cherished and loved. And the origins of this interest clearly went back to Omega days, showing a touch of Picasso's cubism (synthetic perhaps rather than the more austerely analytical) combined with Matisse's secure sense of the blandishments of colour. Edward in public showed only this strand of his work in a safely respectable, endistanced way connected with decoration – consider, for example, the painted wooden tray from around 1926 which has turned up in several Omega exhibitions. The 1967 show seems to have been the first time that he consented to exhibit abstract paintings, but that the impulse had been there from the beginning, and had been rather secretively satisfied, can scarcely be doubted.

At the time of his absorption into the Omega/Bloomsbury circle, Edward was already exhibiting, though it is not now very clear exactly what. His first appearance before the public was apparently in the 1918 show of the London Group, which took place in the Mansard Gallery of Heal's progressive furniture store. The Group had been started four years before as a way of showing art by some of the younger British artists who were

8

already indicating the influence of the Cubists, and as well as the leading young independents it included a group of refugees from Omega who had for one reason or another quarrelled with Roger Fry. At the time feelings had run high, fanned by the trouble-making propensities in Wyndham Lewis, the principal dissident, but aided also by Fry's dictatorial ways. Now the fuss had died down a bit, partly because, with the war reaching its final stages, there seemed to be something more important to worry about than the personal disagreements of people who in various ways were all bent on dragging British art out of Victoria's reign and into the light of modern day. Indeed, in the summer of 1918 Roger Fry himself and Nina Hamnett were both exhibiting in Heal's along with some of Fry's erstwhile enemies.

In fact, at this point there was in practice an astonishing degree of interchangeability among the various groups and eccentric individuals in the London art world. It was perfectly possible for a lively newcomer like Edward to make contact with many different interests which generally all proved ultimately to be interconnecting, because of shared histories and training, or intellectual sympathy, or unpredictable personal liking, or simply the existence of common ground in the salons of such as the overwhelming Lady Ottoline Morrel, artistic lion-hunter extraordinary. It is recorded that the first time Lady Ottoline set eyes on Edward she was whisking out of a lavatory he was about to enter at the Omega; she stopped momentarily, stared at him, said 'So you're the new artist. I see, how interesting' and moved on.

Subsequently, he was invited frequently to her country house parties at Garsington. Edward also became friendly with Augustus John and his group, and took a particular liking to Dorelia, long Augustus's favourite model and mistress, and at this time engaged in a lengthy and stormy affair with the painter Henry Lamb. This affection came in useful when the rich Chilean painter Alvaro Guevara, all-purpose Latin lover to London art and society, took a fancy to Edward after seeing some of his work, carried him off to his studio and proceeded enthusiastically to proposition him: not eager to accept, Edward insisted that he was already committed to a hopeless love of Dorelia, and so made good his escape to Dodie in Maida Vale. He had a similar close shave with the similarly bisexual Duncan Grant, bright star among the already established painters of Bloomsbury; but Grant, not at all put out by rejection, became a lifelong friend.

It was obviously to some extent due to his personal charm, but much more to the quality perceived in his work, that Edward soon became a familiar figure in the more advanced exhibitions of the time. In the show of paintings at the Omega Gallery in October 1918 he was the largest single contributor, with nine canvasses on view, and on the whole the critics approved, though they were quick to note influences in his draughtsmanship from Modigliani and Gaudier-Brzeska, which were very usual among Omega-connected artists at that time and may well have been imbibed indirectly. For the moment Edward was high in Fry's estimation – and not just for his candle-shades: Fry also bought some of his drawings for his own collection, and included a reproduction of one of them in an influential article he wrote, 'Line as a Means of Expression in Modern Art', in the

9

10

11

12

13

*Burlington Magazine* of December 1918. At the same time Edward was invited to contribute a print to *Woodcuts by Various Artists*, an Omega publication (taken over from Virginia and Leonard Woolf's Hogarth Press after a disagreement over artistic control) in which he figured alongside Fry, Grant, Vanessa Bell and McKnight Kauffer, best remembered as the wizard of the London Underground poster.

Edward was to show again with the London Group the following year, by which time Fry had moved into the group and was well on the way to taking over, a process he would complete in a year or two, pushing his enthusiasm for French art as a model, to the exclusion of anyone who did not share it. When Picasso and Derain visited London in 1918 in connection with a season of the Diaghilev Ballet for which they had both designed productions, they went to the London Group Show and Derain picked out Fry's paintings as the best (compared to what? one might ask) without knowing who had painted them, while Picasso, well-known for his low opinion of British art, tactfully held his peace. It is not recorded what, if anything, these Paris luminaries thought of Edward's work, but in any event he was probably not too concerned, since he continued to gather good opinions with his appearances in mixed shows like that which took place at Omega immediately after the opening of the revelatory 1918 Diaghilev season. In it Edward showed a portrait of Barclay Donne, Dodie, and was first recognised as a possible addition to the short list of distinguished new portraitists in Britain after the War.

This, in particular, led on to what was to be one of his most important early commissions. Encouraged by Fry, the novelist and influential literary critic Arnold Bennett had the idea of commissioning Edward to paint a portrait of his wife. Unfortunately it turned out that Mrs Bennett had a deep dislike of having her portrait painted at all, by Edward or anyone else. But Bennett felt bad about this disappointment for Edward, and instead commissioned a portrait of himself. This, of course, was a considerable feather in a young painter's cap, and everything seemed to be going swimmingly for Edward: visits to Garsington and Charleston, regular showings, developing friendships with many prominent people, not only among his fellow artists, but in literary circles like that of the scandalously advanced Sitwells, especially Osbert.

Then misfortune struck. The great scourge of the year immediately after the end of the war was a particularly dangerous strain of Asian flu – the same which killed Egon Schiele at the age of 28. In February 1919 Edward was also stricken, so badly that for a while there were serious fears for his life. When he began to recover he took stock and decided he would like to return to South Africa, at least for long enough to recuperate. For one thing, it would provide a chance of exiting gracefully from his increasingly uncomfortable relationship with Dodie Donne. For another, he could not help noticing that even with the amount of attention he had received while still only 22, he remained terribly poor. While he was in hospital Osbert Sitwell used to bring him piles of review copies of new art books, hopeful that they would interest and distract him, but also well aware that he could sell them in order to pay some of the bills. Decidedly, a breathing space was in order. All his friends seemed to agree, and Roger Fry even set about raising money for his passage back, though very regretful to see the most brilliant new recruit to the now moribund Omega Workshops leaving. When they closed in July 1919 it was no more than bowing to financial inevitability, plus the fact that Fry no longer had the time or the energy to do everything himself.

By that time his main helpmate was already well on his way back to South Africa and, hopefully, renewed health, his way assisted by the money raised from his first one-man show. This, admittedly, was more or less a private affair, sponsored by Maynard Keynes, economist, lover of Duncan Grant and future husband of Lydia Lopokova, who had just enchanted London for the first time in the Diaghilev Ballet season. It was held in Keynes's Gordon Square home. Still, it was satisfying as a sign of progress, and sent Edward off with a lot to think about. He was hardly more than a boy, just turned 22, and he had his whole future to plan. South Africa or England, new worlds to conquer or the old familiar scenes to cherish? He hardly knew, but the first necessity was to get well, get working again and see what developed.

## III

Matisse was the early modern master whose work above all affected Edward Wolfe. To begin with the influence came to him by way of Roger Fry and Fry's teaching – not to mention the directions (orders would be too harsh a word) that Fry used to give the anonymous workers at his Omega Workshops. Matisse had figured modestly in Fry's first Post-Impressionist show in London, 1910-11, where his three paintings and miscellaneous works in other media made him, in the opinion of one notable, not unsympathetic critic, C.J. Holmes, 'the enigma of the show, even for artists and critics'. In Fry's Second Post-Impressionist Exhibition of 1912, he took a dominating role, with no fewer than nineteen major paintings. This was, of course, four years before Edward arrived to study art in England, but he can hardly have been unaware of the enormous influence exerted by the Matisse paintings on Duncan Grant, Vanessa Bell and other painters in the Bloomsbury ambience – particularly *La Danse*, the great rhythmic circle of naked female dancers against a background of blue and green which had inspired several British copies and emulations.

He can never have expected that he would come into much closer and more direct contact with Matisse's work than ever before on board the ship which carried him away from European art circles and towards South Africa. Among his fellow-passengers were two with whom he struck up an immediate friendship, a South African tycoon called Brandon Davis and his wife. Despite his bluff and businesslike exterior, Davis proved to be a passionate enthusiast for modern art, and Matisse in particular. He had in fact gone to a Matisse exhibition in Europe, been so carried away that he bought up half of it (a slight exaggeration, perhaps) and was shipping his spoils back to South Africa, where they would be the first examples of Matisse's art to burst upon an unsuspecting Johannesburg.

Wolfe.

Such enthusiasm, for such a subject, could not but charm Edward, and his friendship with the Davises was rapidly cemented into a lasting relationship through which they became his greatest friends and patrons in South Africa. (Later on Davis settled in London and, introduced to the art dealer Freddie Mayor by Edward, put up finance for the Mayor Gallery, where Edward frequently showed. Later still he killed himself.)

Naturally the Davis collection gave Edward a valuable opportunity to study Matisse at first hand, and learn the lessons of his vibrant colours, his strong outlines and the powerful interior tensions which strengthened his sometimes rather casual-seeming compositions. Edward even became, for a short while, the proud owner of a major Matisse – a portrait of a woman which a friend of Davis's managed to spoil for him by dubbing it 'Squint-Eyed Lizzie'. Consequently (or so he insisted), he felt impelled to hand it over to Edward, to do what he would with it. Though Edward liked it very much, he felt he could not afford to keep it, and so eventually he handed it over to Roger Fry to sell for him, with the result that he received the then princely sum of £500 to finance his first trip to Paris. But that was three years on, when he had returned to Europe.

Meanwhile, Edward was settling in to build up his strength after his long bout of influenza. The sun and the warmth helped – throughout his life he was a sun-baby, and never felt he got enough in England, either for his physical well-being or for his painting. And he was reunited with that redoubtable lady, his mother, who was at this time living in Johannesburg, and if not exactly a traditional, restful image of motherliness, was at least bound and determined to look after anyone who came within range and seemed to need it – not least, certainly, her own son. He was also feeling strong enough to start work again, and when he found that his old art teacher, George Smithard, had died while he was in England, contrived to rent the studio from Smithard's widow.

Once in the midst of renewed activity as a painter, he improved by leaps and bounds. He had decided now to return to England as soon as he decently could, and arranged to have a one-man show of his work early in 1920 at Leon Levson's Johannesburg gallery to raise money for the return trip. The show was quite successful, and through it he met several other people who were to be important friends in the future: the painter Enslin du Plessis, for instance, and the writer of children's books Ethel Hayman, for whom he did a series of watercolour illustrations for her 'Prudence Elizabeth' stories. Another new friend was William Plomer, the poet and novelist, who at the time of their meeting was a surprisingly cool and clear-eyed 17-year-old. He has left us a vivid picture of the young Edward Wolfe in his autobiography *Double Lives*:

> Slight in stature, with a Byzantine face under a heavy black fringe and gifted with a wonderful gaity and childlike zest for life, he made his own world and lived in it... His work and his talk and the vivid environment which, like a bower-bird, he had created for himself refreshed my eyes and spirit and easily lured me away from the tennis parties and coming-out dances.

Edward, he concludes, 'had, as one might say, talent as a character.'

15

Fortified with the financial results of his Johannesburg show, Edward was all ready to leave for London when some other new friends, the violinist Zelma Whitehouse and her husband, introduced him to a new realm of visual experience by taking him to the gold mines of Village Deep. He was so excited by what he saw there that he decided to postpone his return until the end of the English winter, and spend some time painting the miners and the landscape. The Whitehouses lent him a house near Village Deep Mine, and he painted in an empty barrack in the native compound. His drawings, says Plomer, 'caught in a flowing line the shapely sadness and exiled vigour of naked black miners', and found in the process a new strength and tension. For all that, his sympathy was generally human rather than strictly political: he was fascinated by the heroic aspect of the miners, their physical beauty and dignity, as he was by the stark shapes of the nearby landscape, something which was recurrently to haunt him for the rest of his life.

Early in 1921 he was finally ready to go back to London and take up his artistic career there again. When he arrived it transpired that his portrait of Arnold Bennett had been so successful and so widely admired that Bennett's wife, Marguerite, had been persuaded to reconsider her earlier doubts in the matter and Bennett now commissioned Edward to paint a portrait of her as a companion-piece to his own. There was also the value of the Matisse he had been given by Brandon Davis to be realized, and again Roger Fry proved helpful. Though the Omega Workshops were by now dead and buried, Fry's personal influence continued to spread: he had virtually taken over the running of the London Group, and his tastes in recent and contemporary art – Van Gogh, Gauguin, Cézanne, Matisse – were rapidly becoming the accepted pantheon for the younger generation of artists, being dominant influences on even those painters who grew restive under Fry's somewhat dictatorial rule and showed signs of breaking away to found splinter groups of their own, like the Seven and Five Society, begun in 1920 while Edward was in South Africa and so called because originally it was supposed to comprise seven painters and five sculptors. Though Edward remained friendly with Fry and his old Bloomsbury friends, he was by no means slavishly attached to them, and managed in the next few years to be friendly and also to exhibit with the rival groups without deeply offending anybody.

For the moment, however, his interests were directed primarily abroad. He had little or no direct experience of Europe and the heady Paris art-world Fry was so enthusiastic about. He wanted to explore for himself, and with the money from the Matisse he determined to take himself off to Paris and stay and paint there as long as his finances permitted. He went early in 1922 with his painter friend Elliott Seabrooke, and rented a studio in Montparnasse, an area then much favoured by impecunious artists and sanctified by the memory of one of Edward's artistic idols, Modigliani, who had died there two years previously at the age of 35. Edward had never had the chance to know Modigliani personally, any more than he had Gaudier-Brzeska, who had been killed in the war a year before he arrived in London. But in both cases he had had ample opportunity to study their work, and imbibe the legends from people who had known them well – Fry in the case of Gaudier-Brzeska, Nina Hamnett in the case of Modigliani.

Now, through Fry and Duncan Grant, he was able to get to know other intimates of the Modigliani circle, particularly the Russian sculptor Zadkine, and also met the Russian emigré painters Larionov and Goncharova, both of whom took on an added magic in his eyes because of their association with the Diaghilev Ballet (Larionov had designed *Contes Russes* and Goncharova *Firebird*). Later he took a studio in the Rue de Seine on the Left Bank, just above the poet Vildreck, and began to strike out on his own, making his own friends. Among these were Claude Maître, head of the Musée Guimet, whom he met at mass one day and who subsequently gave him one of his most treasured possessions, a big stone head of Buddha.

Through Claude Maître he met and became friendly also with Roger Désormière, just a year older than himself and then at the beginning of a distinguished musical career which would soon include musical directorship of the Ballets Suédois and the Ballet Russe in their most innovative Twenties phase. For the first time Edward had the feeling of being close to the intellectual centre of things, and found that he was in his element.

His stay in Paris was brought to an end by another bout of illness, which forced him to

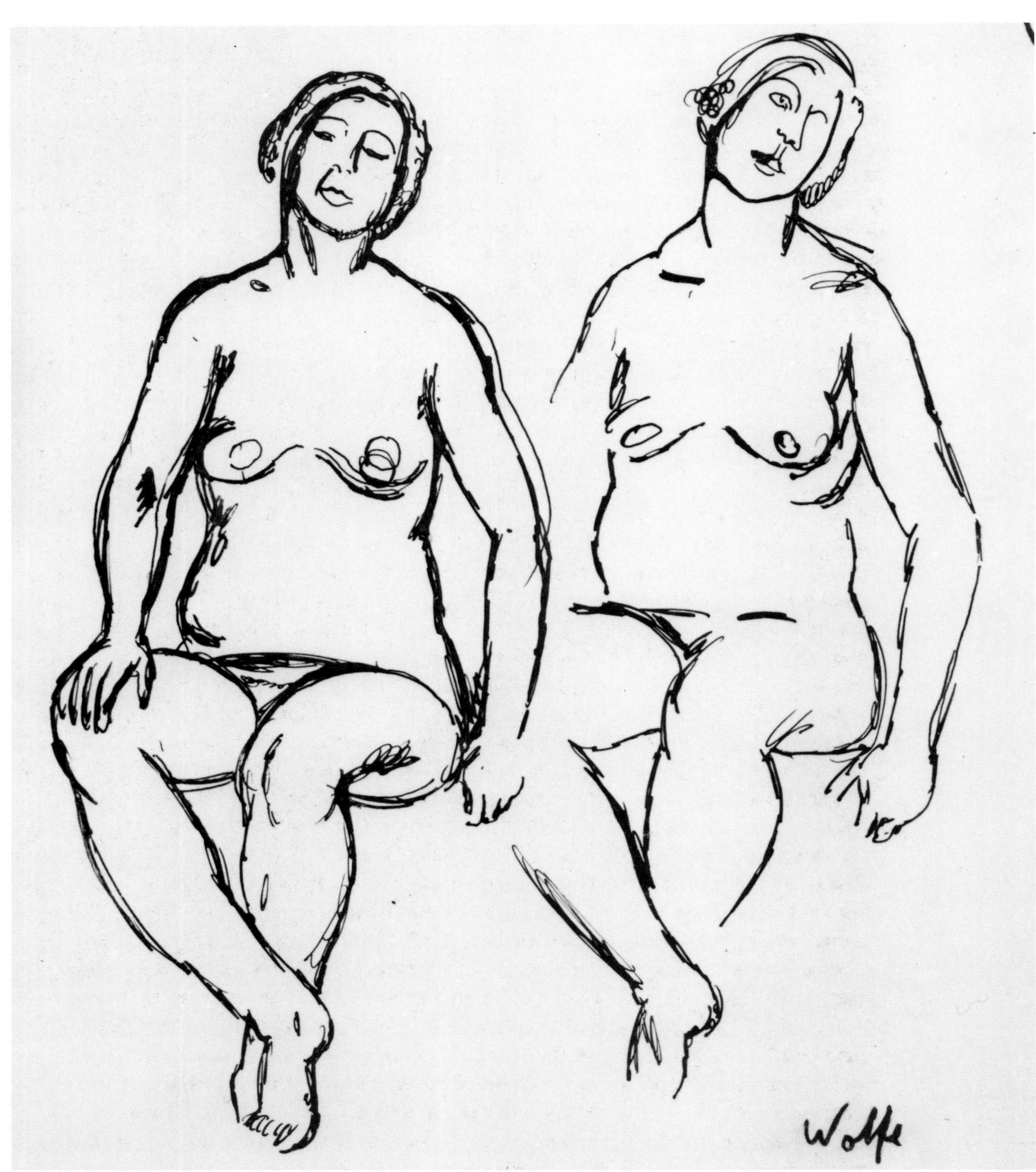


16

17

18

19

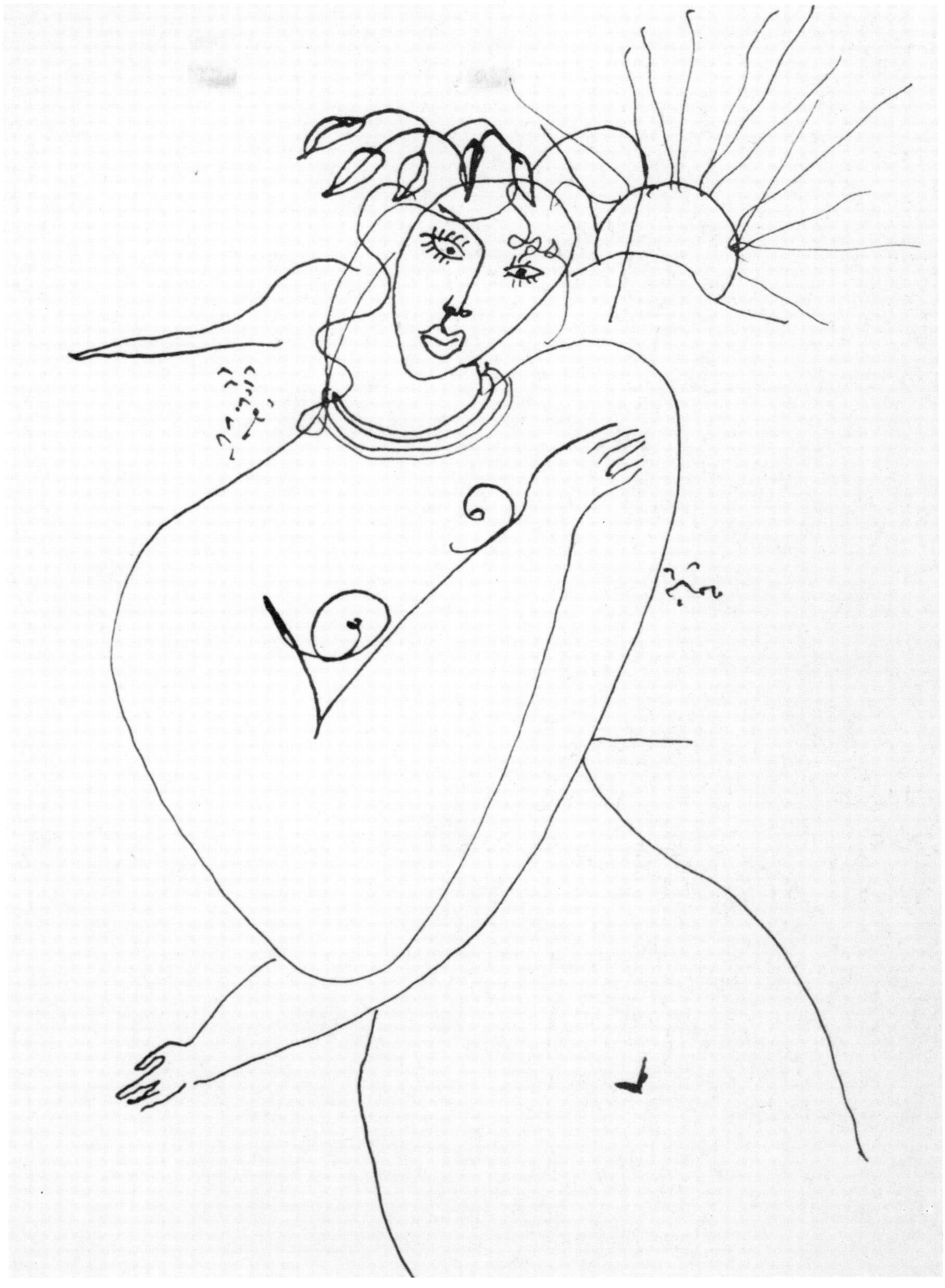

go south to warmer climes. In fact, despite his tremendous vitality, he fought a constant battle with illnesses of various kinds throughout his life, many of his ailments, particularly his heart problems later on, very probably the legacy of his Asiatic flu in 1919. However, this time the illness was possibly something of a blessing in disguise, since he responded passionately and immediately to the vivid colours of Spain and her people. One of the first visible results of this was his painting *The Spanish Girl*, which was one of the great successes of the Venice Biennale in 1923 and was bought there by Arnold Bennett, who was by now one of his most fervent admirers.

After Spain, Italy was next on his cultural itinerary. An emotional itinerary also, as it turned out, since it was while he was living in Florence in 1923 that he went through one of his formative sentimental experiences, one that hit him harder than anything up to then, driving him, most uncharacteristically (and briefly!) to contemplate suicide. In Florence he found himself rapidly in the midst of a highly sophisticated, cultivated and cosmopolitan society where all kinds of sexual variations were at least tolerated, if not enthusiastically practised. Among those he got to know there were Norman Douglas, Charles Scott Montcrieff (best known as the first English translator of Proust), Aldous Huxley and Carlo Loser, art collector (his collection was particularly rich in Cézannes) and musical patron.

He also met what he later claimed was the great love of his life – or two of them, to be precise. The first was the New York millionaire Henry Costa, who represented in many ways Edward's social and erotic ideal, and with whom he proceeded to have a passionate affair. The second was a slightly older woman, Countess Byba, with whom Edward, never one to observe tiresome limitations in his tastes, fell madly in love, and she, apparently, with him, though most of her previous experiences had been lesbian. At which point he made the cardinal error of introducing his two lovers, and even throwing them together, so eager was he that they should like each other. The predictable result was that they got on all too well – so well that they decided to marry – and Edward found himself left out in the cold. Deeply hurt, he just took a train to Rome, without telling anyone what he was doing, and set about recovering the best way he knew, by painting out his grief. Among the first results was one of his best self-portraits, not, it must be said, particularly tragedy-struck in appearance, even though Edward later affirmed that if he had not painted it then he would have killed himself.

But he was young and resilient, and soon began making more friends in Rome, including the painter/caricaturist Edmund X. Kapp and his wife Yvonne Cloud. After three months he went back to Florence, refreshed and restored, and stayed there until 1925, when he returned to London.

In London he found the situation if anything more advantageous to him than when he had left. The London Group continued, and continued to provide him with a convenient outlet for his work. But also the Seven and Five Society was going from strength to strength, and each yearly exhibition showed more distinguished new members with vaguely avant-garde leanings. In December 1923 Ben Nicholson joined, and at the next

20

show in January 1926 were added, as well as Edward, Winifred Nicholson, Ben's first wife, Evie Hone the Irish stained-glass artist and Jessica Dismorr, among others. Edward's joining the rival organization does not seem, though, to have turned Roger Fry against him. In 1926, on Fry's insistence, he became a member of the London Artists' Association, a curious sort of sponsored co-operative founded and masterminded financially by Maynard Keynes, which was designed to give the chosen artists a basic income (£150 a year) and sell their work for them, the initial salary to be treated as an advance against their percentage (70%) of any sales made, while the Association's percentage commission went to keep the kitty in a healthy condition. In its first five years of life the Association was a great success, thanks partly to the economic knowhow of Keynes and partly to the artistic influence of Fry, which had enabled it to sell some 700 works for about £22,000. Certainly at this juncture in his career membership brought solid advantages to Edward, and when in 1926 he had his first one-man London show at a real gallery (the Mayor Gallery) his position was such as many young painters of his age – not yet thirty – might well have envied.

Not that he necessarily did the most businesslike things to maintain and improve it: as William Plomer, a friend re-found in London (Edward painted a splendidly owlish portrait of him in 1926), had already observed, he tended to live in his own world rather than the less comfortable, more practical world around him; he was totally uninterested in money and status *per se*, and the soul of a wanderer kept him almost constantly on the move, sometimes for brief painting trips (to Spain and Morocco in 1928, for instance), and sometimes for years at a time, as in his 'Mexican period', which started with six months in New York (1934) and continued for another eighteen in Taxco, Mexico, where he rented a house and just painted, far geographically and psychologically from his many contacts in England and the London galleries.

One thing, though, was fairly clearly established by the mid-Twenties, and that was his style. He succeeded miraculously in never being trapped in it or closed to other influences, from art or from life, but from very early on his paintings and drawings were instantly recognisable, and the clear lines of continuity remained to the end of his professional life. We have remarked that the first influences he underwent on his arrival from South Africa in 1916 were those of Gaudier-Brzeska, Modigliani and Matisse, probably in that order. Gaudier-Brzeska, the 'savage messiah' of Jim Ede's biography and Ken Russell's film, was, as the label implies, one of the most important apostles of primitive art in the somewhat refined purlieus of British painting and sculpture immediately before the First World War. Primarily a sculptor himself, he designed textiles and ceramics for the Omega Workshops and managed thus to domesticate and familiarize buyers with certain traits – a sometimes wilful distortion of form, a bold stylization of line and colour – which they would certainly have found much harder to accept in the context of traditional fine art. Also, which Edward particularly appreciated and learned from, he was a master draughtsman, embodying tremendous energy in a minimum of apparently casual, improvised lines.

Modigliani, Nina Hamnett's friend and hero, was a much more purely painterly influence. He showed to the full Gaudier-Brzeska's enthusiasm for tribal art, especially Oceanic, but he had turned it to very different ends, evolving his own highly mannered style of drawing and painting in which the people he usually painted were reduced to flat patterns, with almond eyes in almond-shaped faces, and bodies made up of gentle, elegant intersecting curves. Though the charm of his work was for some years after his death a mystery to most British art-lovers (Edward's great friend Osbert Sitwell being a prominent exception), a number of artists loved and understood it, notably the sculptor Jacob Epstein, who had known Modigliani well and spent much time with him. But Edward also responded intensely, in his own way, and some of the conventions of portraiture invented or adopted by Modigliani became for ever a recognisable part of his own visual language.

It is doubtful if he could ever have been an uncritical imitator of Modigliani – or anyone else – his way of working and thinking was too innately independent for that. But certainly as he moved through the Twenties and Thirties the influence of Modigliani, which could easily prove enervating to those who simply took over his tricks without his reasons for them, was strongly and for the better modified by that of Matisse. Temperamentally, Edward, with his 'childlike zest for life', was much closer to Matisse, and the intense, vibrant colour which was the life of Matisse's canvases also captivated the 'little African savage' in Edward. Already in his early paintings the colours take on a strange autonomous life of their own, creating a bold pattern of interrelated planes which seems to coexist happily with the forms outlined by his crisp and confident draughtsmanship (that 'flowing line' Plomer early approved of) yet remains at the same time oddly independent of them, as though two different pictures are fused together in the forge of the artist's vision. This effect undoubtedly arises from a genuine like-mindedness between Edward and Matisse rather than slavish imitation, and this remains true even when, as in some of the Moroccan scenes and characters he painted in 1928, the subject-matter is noticeably similar to some of Matisse's early work.

These three influences, plus Edward's African background and penchant for travelling and working abroad, must make him sound like rather an exotic on the British art scene. And so in a sense he was, but not so decisively as one might suppose. For one thing, he was by no means the only painter in London during the Twenties to undergo the same influences, and somehow the British (for that in his professional formation, training and experience Edward essentially was) found their own distinctive way of absorbing and naturalizing the ideas and apprehensions of the Post-Impressionists and Fauves. There is a certain kind of English stolidity and sobriety which successfully tamed and acclimatised the wilder elements to the depiction of foursquare London suburbs even before Edward arrived in Britain, in the work of the so-called Camden Town Group and other followers of Sickert. And that same sobriety and level, appraising gaze is quite definitely present in many of Edward's best portraits and in the landscapes, whether of Tangier or Wales, Southern Ireland or South Africa. In both portraits and landscapes he shows a surprising awareness of the skull beneath the skin, the structure of stones and bones which gives the surface its character and resonance. Sometimes his critics have thrown words like 'decorative' at him as though they are terms of abuse. But while he has few equals in British art for sheer sensuous enjoyment of surfaces – one must look to Hockney for another so happy, unrepentent sensualist – there is a strength and solidity underneath which give his work staying-power: his are paintings which reveal more and more the longer one lives with them, rather than so many pretty faces which have exhausted their interest almost before the honeymoon is over.

It is this feeling of fusion at a high temperature and under pressure which endows Edward's work with its distinctive power and excitement – unique in the milieu from which he sprang: Duncan Grant, for instance, with whom he is in many respects closely comparable, tended always to keep 'decorative' and 'serious' work in separate compartments, and while one is always at liberty to prefer, as most would do now, the elegant, exotic decorations to the rather drab, slogging canvases in which he dutifully proclaimed his debt to Cézanne, the pity is that one so often has to make a choice between desirable qualities rather than finding them indissolubly linked. In Edward's art, though he was always an intelligent painter rather than a happy primitive, he does not seem conscious of making a choice, or forcing us to do so: the paintings, good or bad, all spring from the same source and the same kind of inspiration.

And there are remarkably few bad ones. Instinct sees to his initial impulses, and he was a natural painter if ever there was one. However skilfully shaped by craft his work may be, it always seems to come out of some internal necessity: one never gets a sense of pot-boiling, and he always seems to have been remarkably incapable of painting for purely financial reasons. Occasionally there may crop up a painting or drawing which apparently comes from no stronger urge than habit – the principal pitfall of the natural, compulsive painter – but even these have the merits as well as the faults of sincerity: he is incapable of pomposity, of dressing up an automatic impulse pretentiously to look like a world-shattering statement. Quite possibly he could have done some of his portrait-drawings of children in his sleep, and it is unlikely that he found all the children of all his friends equally inspiring as subject-matter. But even here he does not temporize and judge the effect: honesty about his own work is sometimes a burden, but he could work no other way.

This seems to have been recognised from very early on in his career: that though worldly in respect of his social life – here was no shrinking recluse needing to work in solitude – Edward was profoundly unworldly in whatever concerned his actual work-processes. In Britain, where sincerity is so often invoked as the touchstone of artistic worth, this gained him more respect among critics and buyers than any display of technical virtuosity could have done, and throughout the interwar years he did consistently well in both areas. Indeed, had he been content to stay put and develop his gallery exposure and his home market in a more consistent fashion he would no doubt have become one of the biggest names in British painting. Instead he continued to follow his own drummer, wherever that unpredictable individual might lead. Not that this was always a problem. His public in Britain could readily understand a painting trip to the Mediterranean and North Africa, such as that he made in 1928 and the results displayed in his one-man show at the Warren Gallery in 1929, since sun-drenched scenes were a readily permitted exoticism, and he continued to gather golden opinions in his one-man show at the London Artists' Association (to which he was still attached) in 1930, and his big Manchester show in 1931.

He was also able to develop another interest – his passion for the theatre – when he attracted the attention of the great theatre manager C.B. Cochran, and was commissioned to do sets and costumes for Cochran's 1931 *Revue* and more for his show *Streamline* in 1932. More substantial, and more completely in accord with his special talents, was the design for set and costumes that he did, on an absolute shoestring, be it said, for Ninette de Valois's version of the Milhaud dance-spectacle, *La Création du Monde,* staged for the Camargo Society in 1931. The work had been originally designed by Léger for the Ballet Suédois in 1923, and embodied in sophisticated form a primitive tribal version of the creation myth. While Léger imparted a somewhat mechanistic, impersonal aspect to his costumes for the participants (even though they also evoked the artefacts of Oceania and of some African tribes), Edward presented a much more organic vision, as though the gods and spirits had grown from the same roots as the primeval forest which surrounded them and provided a background for their ritual.

Oddly enough, for a painter who was an actor once, there is little or nothing that could be called 'theatrical' in Edward's painting, then or subsequently, but he could have been a superb theatrical designer, and it is a thousand pities that he did not have more opportunities to exercise this particular talent. The setting for James Laver's play, *The Heart Was Not Burned* (about Keats, Shelley and Byron) in 1938 was the only further substantial piece of theatre design he was ever asked to do. Nor did what is in many artists a kindred talent for decorating books find much outlet: a frontispiece for a limited edition of John Collier's story *Green Thoughts* in 1932 and some drawings for small volumes by poet friends during the Forties were about all that ever saw the light of day, and his most substantial and beautiful work in that line, the sumptuous series of colour compositions inspired by Louis Golding's new translation of *The Song of Songs* in 1930 when Edward was working in Tangier, were not actually published (in a portfolio) until the Eighties.

In 1934, after staying relatively fixed in Britain, if not necessarily London, for the better part of ten years, Edward decided that it was time to start his travels again. Certainly his recurrent need to seek the sun had something to do with it, but also his natural restlessness. Probably also there were more personal, emotional, reasons behind the move, as there had been behind his return to South Africa in 1919, and his precipitate flight from Florence to Rome in 1924. He had for some years been living mostly with his mother, who had come over in 1926 and with typical energy and determination set up a boarding house in Clanricarde Gardens, Bayswater, to provide a stable home for herself and Edward and a little financial security into the bargain. On the whole Edward seems to

21

22

24

25

26

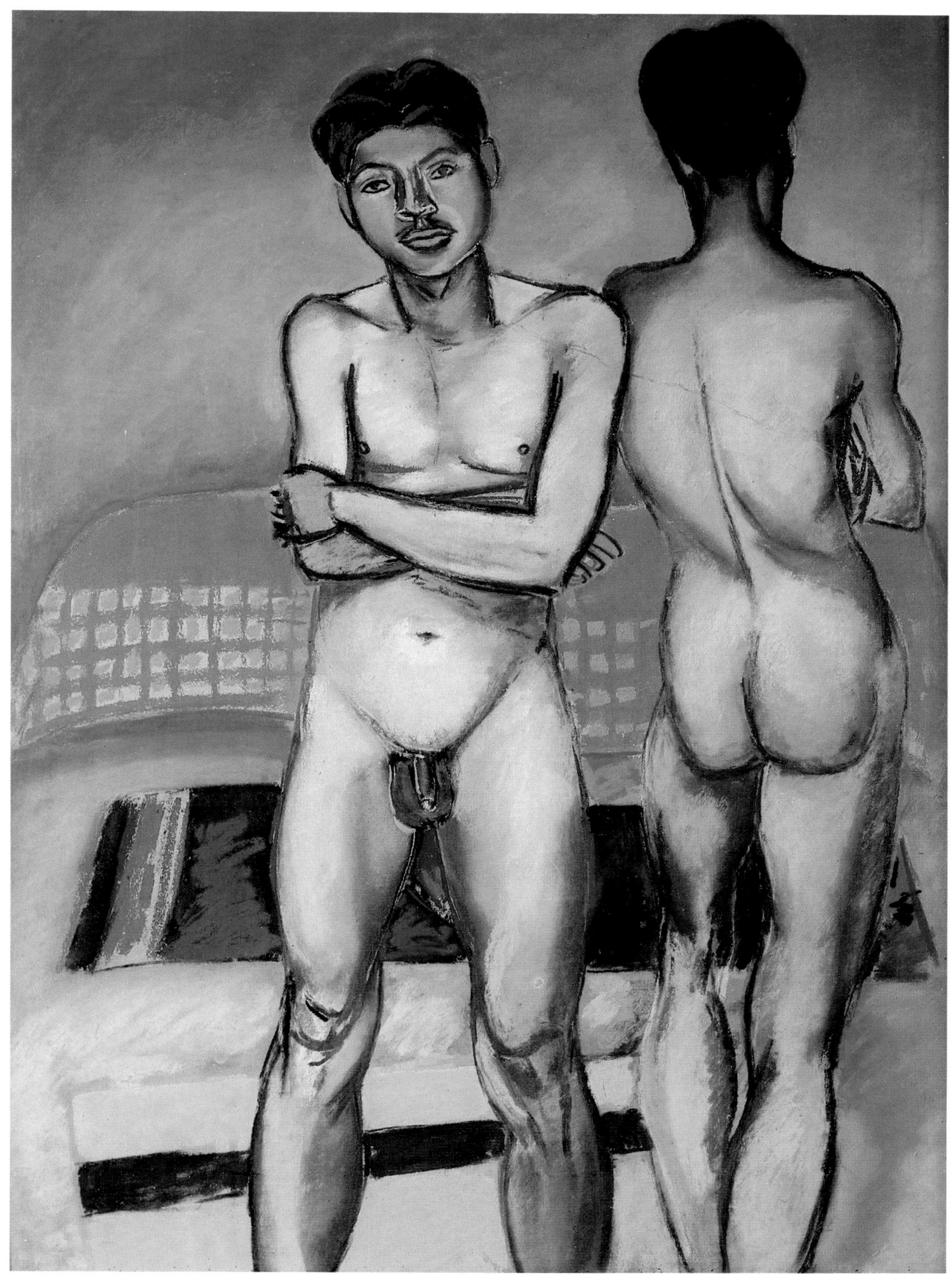

27

23

28

have got on well with his mother, who quite cheerfully accepted her background role in his life, though given occasionally to picturesque complaint: once she told John Collier 'It's sitting in the front row of the opera I should be, wearing pearls, instead of cooking for *him* and his friends.' Undoubtedly sometimes he found the situation constricting, especially when he felt the need to spread his wings emotionally and sexually.

The early Thirties were in fact the period of his two most lasting, physical relationships with women, both of which came to rather unfortunate ends. First, he conceived a powerful attachment to one of his favourite models, a girl called Marcelle, and moved away from his mother to live with her. The relationship went very well for a while, but then they went to a party where Marcelle met the writer Peter Quennell. It was the *coup de foudre,* and she left Edward flat for Quennell, much to his distress and lasting sense of grievance. The other woman in his life around this time, Bridget, he also painted frequently and had a passionate affair with, attracted seemingly by her colourful personality and an undefinably exciting sense of danger about her. This latter alas became all too definable, when she became involved in Black Magic, was drawn, like so many before her, into the circle of Aleister Crowley, and eventually killed herself.

These two unfortunate experiences no doubt gave Edward strong negative reasons for getting out of Britain for a while, in addition to the more positive ones of wanting to seek new experiences in new places and give himself new challenges as an artist. In mid-1934 he took himself off to New York, with no very definite plans in mind except that it was intended to be a stopping-place merely, on his way to the sun, which he meant to seek out before New York's bitter winter descended. He enjoyed New York, the social whirl and the eagerness and openness of the Americans he met there. But his heart was really set on Mexico, and at the onset of winter he headed southward, ending up in Taxco, where he was fascinated by the dry desert heat, so beneficial to his health, the stark desert landscape, with its exotic cacti and rough-hewn rock formations, and the picturesquely dressed but rather mysterious peasants, whom he felt to be repositories of an old, pre-Columbian past which remained inviolable beneath their superficial friendliness.

Here he stayed for eighteen months. It is evident from the rather harsh ungainly forms which appear in his art during his time in Mexico that not only did he respond in the most direct possible way to the specific characteristics of the Mexican landscape and people, but he was fully conscious of what was going on in Mexican art of the time, particularly the violent, extrovert political murals of Orozco, Rivera and Siqueiros. These might seem like an unlikely influence on an artist nurtured in the refinement of Bloomsbury. Though the influence was only a passing phase, absorbed and forgotten when Edward returned to England, it does remind us that, whatever his artistic beginnings, Edward was emphatically not a delicate, refined artist. As Bryan Robertson well put it at the time of Edward's Arts Council retrospective in 1967:

> Edward Wolfe is from Africa and he has brought a temperament conditioned by scorching sun and blinding light to bear upon the protected interiors and muted light

29

30

31

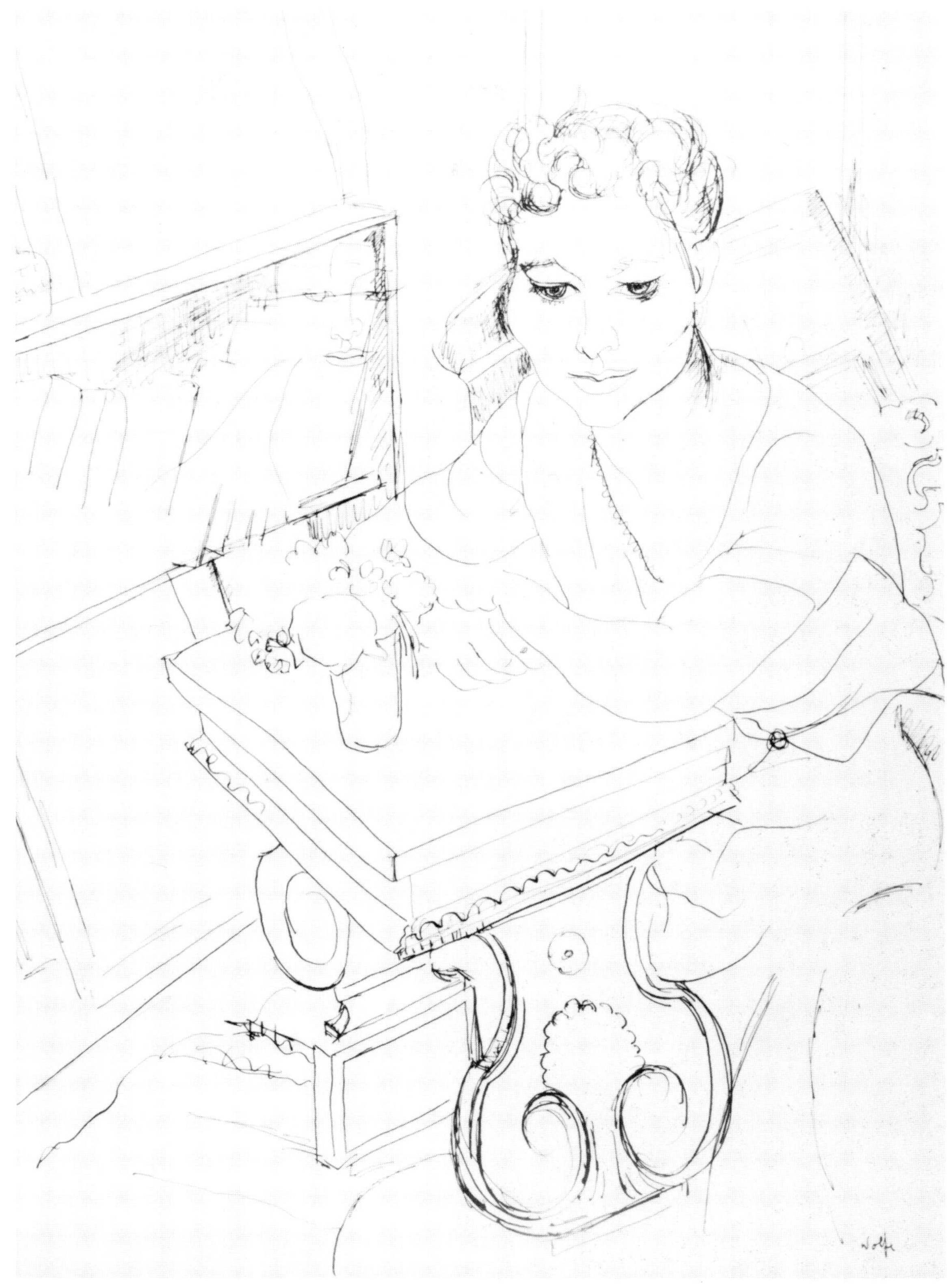

> of Europe. The result is not fine-grained but coarse, tough, harsh – and radiant. We do not know such radiance; we are not used, with all our awareness and sophistication, to this intensity of raw colour.

Edward would no doubt have stayed longer in Mexico, well content as he was with the place and the sales he was making to visiting Americans without ever going near a gallery, but he was informed that his mother was suffering from inoperable cancer, and felt he must be with her. Back in England he found that his uningratiating, uncompromising Mexican pictures were sometimes looked at rather askance by his old admirers, but all the same his one-man show at the Lefevre Gallery in 1936 was a decided success, and at his 1938 show at the Mayor Gallery he was given a further leg-up the ladder to Establishment acceptance when one of his Irish landscapes, a harmony in vivid greens called *Laughane, Spring* was bought by Mrs Joan Jameson and presented by her to the Tate Gallery. By this time the war-clouds were again gathering over Europe, and a period of considerable frustration, personal and artistic, was about to commence for Edward. This was the more unfortunate in that as he entered his forties (in 1937) he felt confident as never before – confident of his talents, and ready to believe for the first time that he might prove not only a hardworking and dedicated artist, but quite possibly a great one.

However, national emergencies have a way of sweeping such personal considerations aside. In 1939, eager to do his bit, Edward joined the First Aid Section of the Chelsea ARP. When the war began, it was impossible for him to be called up, on account both of his age and his health, but he was very eager to become an official War Artist. Unfortunately here – or so he always believed – one of the few enemies he had made intervened to block his path. Somewhere along the line he seems to have got on the wrong side of Kenneth Clark, who had in the war years a position of unequalled power as a 'maker and breaker'. He could, had he wished, have had Edward made a war artist in a moment. But he did not wish, and Edward subsequently maintained, at least in his more depressed moments, that Clark had broken him. He would be aware of and resent such things, for though he was in most respects not very practical or good at selling himself in a buyers' market, he was in an odd way quite career-minded, and felt any slight, real or imagined, intensely, since they all fuelled his self-doubts and the lack of confidence engendered by his sketchy-to-non-existent education.

In the event, the war years were to prove a hiatus in his career and a sad blow to his hitherto quite steady progress. He was injured in a car accident in Chelsea, being propelled right through the windscreen of a car he was not driving, and went to Dorset to recover, playing his part in the war effort, rather improbably, by becoming a coastguard at Chideock, where his old and much-painted friend Jet Fairley had a cottage which he and his mother, much weakened but still hanging on, could use. It was at Chideock that Mrs Wolfe finally died, and later in 1940 Edward joined the BBC, though not in any noticeably creative capacity: his precise function was as Staff Welfare Officer at Evesham. The next year he moved to Bristol, still with the BBC, where he, the least censorious of

32

33

34

35

36

37

men, was given a job as censor. He still kept up some contacts with the London art world of pre-war days, now scattered, and in 1943 arranged an exhibition of the London Group at the Victoria Art Gallery, Bath. In June 1944, when things were getting back to something nearer normal in the London galleries, he had a show in London at the Redfern Gallery which he shared with drawings by Segonzac and etchings by Manet.

Finally in 1945, after victory in Europe, he felt free to leave the BBC and return full-time to painting. A working tour of Wales brought him to the artists' settlement-cum-architectural folly of Portmeirion, where he met the place's creator Clough Williams-Ellis. Williams-Ellis took to him and offered him the village's toy town hall as a studio. This offer he gratefully accepted, and painted there regularly for nearly three years, gradually working himself out of his wartime depression and making contact again with the only thing that really mattered to him, his art. He was also able to travel again, after the inevitable wartime restrictions, and in 1946 had a very productive painting trip to Ischia, the results of which were shown at the end of the year in the Florida Gallery, Naples. He was also invited to contribute to a show of British and American paintings at the American Art Centre in New York, and began to renew his international contacts.

By 1948, 'broken' or not, he seemed to be back in full form, and had a succession of successful one-man shows in London at the Lefevre, the Mayor and the O'Hana galleries, in Paris at the Galerie de Seine and in 1950 on an extensive tour of the British provinces. In his mid-fifties he was willy-nilly becoming part of the art Establishment he so doubted and mistrusted, though his work showed no diminution of boldness and independence thereby. In 1956 he again felt the urge to take time out from Britain, and after this long lapse of time – 35 years – decided to return to his childhood home, South Africa.

Whether it was curiosity that drove him, or nostalgia, or thirst for the sun, or just the promise of a one-man show in Johannesburg, with more possibly to follow, it is difficult now to say. But certainly the effect of the long-unfamiliar scenes on his art was electrifying. He had always had a special feeling for landscape, arising from a deep respect for the natural harmony of nature, so that he had little interest in analysing, like Cézanne or the Cubists, the underlying structure or rearranging the elements into more satisfyingly decorative patterns, but rather felt bound to penetrate to the soul of a particular place by meticulous recording of the given facts and his own highly sensitive responses to them. Curiously, if his British landscapes brought in, instinctively, a certain 'African' wildness and even stridency of colour, his African landscapes stand out in his work as among the most restrained and 'English' of his paintings: relatively subdued in colour and unemphatic in composition, they suggest an unsuspected kinship between him and the played-down, muted landscapes of Euston Road painters like William Coldstream and pre-abstract Victor Pasmore.

When he returned to Britain in 1958 he was painting with renewed vigour and undiminished skill. Immediately on his arrival in London he found a new studio by the Thames at Rotherhithe, and rapidly integrated himself into the new and unfamiliar

38

community. He took to painting very sketchy, immediate impressions of the river scenes outside his window, using oils so diluted that the effect is often like that of a very large, freely handled watercolour. One would never have called him an Impressionist before, but there is certainly something of true Impressionism in this seizing of the moment on canvas before it flies. On the other hand, there is enough of his legacy from the Fauves remaining to ensure that the colours are often quite unrealistic, and so one thinks instead of some of the German painters of early Expressionism, such as August Macke or Franz Marc. The developments of the late Fifties and early Sixties are astonishing for a man nearing seventy, and were carried abroad into his view of foreign parts, long familiar or totally new to him, that he visited and painted throughout the Sixties – including Spain, France, Italy, Tunisia, Gozo and Greece, as well as regular trips to his beloved Wales.

During these years he exhibited regularly with the London Group and in the Royal Academy Summer Exhibitions. And in 1961 a new stability came into his life when he met the Irish writer James O'Connor, who was to be the constant companion and support of his later years. In 1967 he was finally elected an Associate of the Royal Academy, and became a full Academician in 1973. With declining health in the 1970s and what he regarded as the damaging necessity of giving up his Rotherhithe studio, he did less formal

39

work, but was seldom without at least a ballpoint or felt-tip in his hand, constantly noting down his vivid responses to the world about him on menus, programmes or any surface to hand.

William Plomer said that as a young man he had 'talent as a character', and in his last years this quality came flooding back into his life; he was a much loved and fiercely loyal friend, a sparkling conversationalist, and an elfin and unpredictable presence at any gathering. He could talk happily about almost anything except himself. When the Arts Council had its long overdue retrospective of his work to mark his seventieth birthday, the basic facts of his life had to be extracted from him, indirectly, over some months. He never saw much use in talking about Art in the abstract – the point was quite simply to do it. When he died in 1982, at the ripe old age of 85, still resolutely refusing to become a Grand Old Man, his passing occasioned remarkably few formal tributes. Rather, there was a personal sense of loss, even in those who knew him very slightly. For all his diminutive stature, he belonged to a generation of giants, and never seemed smaller than the tallest.

40

## IV

Whichever way you look at it, Edward Wolfe was a maverick in British art. Of course, it might be maintained that he did not belong in British art at all, and seemed odd and unpredictable merely because he was foreign. There is probably something in that, but it does not go very far as an explanation. In his family background – all of it that really counted – he was British, and so he was in his training and the general context of his professional life. True, the influences which shaped him were mostly foreign, but so they were for most of his contemporaries in Britain – there were very few weird enough, like Stanley Spencer, to be wholly self-defining. Indeed, compared with Spencer, Wolfe was a model of conventionality, as an artist and as a man, and if the overtones of a word like maverick suggest a bucking, rearing, ungovernable monster, then it could hardly be much further from the truth.

And yet, invincibly strange and individual he was, in his own devious and subtle ways, so as not to give offence. Right from the start, he created his own world about him, and others could enter it only on his terms. If people liked his painting, it had to be for what it was, not what it might be: he developed at his own pace, in his own direction, and nobody and nothing was going to deflect him. It was no use expecting him to be a technical innovator, or wanting him to tone down his colours into respectability. It was no good requiring him to prove his seriousness by carrying out exercises within the approved standards of dullness, for he was unimpressed. Beneath the impish sense of humour and the social charm there was invincible will and determination, and the less it was founded on natural self-confidence, the more invincible it became.

In fact, he would be a difficult painter to take if he were not, on the level of unthinking sensuous responses, so very easy. Whatever else he may be, he is undoubtedly a colourist, one of those British artists who yearn for the warm south and keep bringing it back for us to light up the drab winter. In a characteristic Wolfe painting, the first thing that hits you, and the last thing you remember, is the colour. It is perfectly possible to stop at the colour, appreciate nothing but the colour, and still have an eminently worthwhile experience. The colour is in a sense the camouflage which allows the rest of what the picture has to say to go unnoticed on a conscious level. But it is never just a sugaring on the pill: it is an essential part of the picture, inseparable from Wolfe's way of looking at things and finding them of interest.

In fact, to call him a decorative artist, as has often been done, is to accept too easily a complete misnomer. It is precisely what he is not, for what is wrong, or insufficient, about merely decorative painting is that it divorces things which should be indissolubly joined together: form and content, the subject of a painting and the way it is painted. In Edward Wolfe's work it all goes together. He was perfectly capable of painting a bad picture – what artist of any worth and enterprise is not? – but he never painted a cheap, shoddy or superficial picture. If he wanted, for example, to paint portraits of beautiful people, so be it. But he never made the mistake of using unbeautiful people as an excuse for beautiful painting – and, to do him justice, he was as capable of painting odd birds like Arnold Bennett or William Plomer and doing it truthfully, as he was of producing a lush nude with the full force of his conviction.

Finally, though it seems an improbable claim, he was a thinking man's painter. His works, however slight and casual-seeming, are thought through; he is never carried away by the superficial sensation, however vivid it may be. There is a certain, call it humility, when the painter is face-to-face with the natural world, a respect for the facts of what is there as well as for the movements of the painter's own sensibility in interpreting those facts. As a portrait-painter and landscape painter he is part of a great tradition – and a specifically British tradition at that. His still-lifes and flower-pieces, among which some of his most compelling work is found, belong rather to the mainstream of European art, and would certainly not exist as they are if it were not for the lessons of the great Impressionists and Post-Impressionists. But even here the tone is individual: Wolfe is certainly not Cézanne, and not even Matisse – nor, admire them as he may, would he wish to be. In the end, a Wolfe is a Wolfe is a Wolfe: immediately recognisable, take it or leave it, and sublimely unconcerned which we finally do.

41

## NOTE ON THE ILLUSTRATIONS

Like many artists, Edward Wolfe possessed a curious mixture of an undirected hoarding instinct and almost complete unconcern for his work once it was finished and done with. Consequently, the survival of early work often seems a matter of whim or sheer blind chance. The earliest definitely datable painting is the *Still Life with Omega Cat* of 1918, which from its inscription may be his first 'official' oil painting, made just after he had left the Slade School. The influences on his early work are already apparent: in the terms of 1918, this is quite moderate modernism, with the solid groundwork of the Slade in draughtsmanship and composition moderated by the rich colour and effective simplification of form he had learnt from Matisse through the teachings of Roger Fry.

During the next few years Wolfe was to move nearer Matisse and further away from the Slade: as the Twenties progress the rhythmic simplifications become bolder, the colours purer and more vivid. In some of the drawings and nude paintings particularly, a dash of Modigliani is added to the mixture: Modigliani's characteristic elongations of the human form, and the almond eyes he gives almost all his portrait subjects, also became part of Wolfe's artistic vocabulary, and were to remain so.

At this time also he did abstracts, though these in general are more difficult to date, since he never exhibited abstract paintings until the Arts Council retrospective of 1967. It is clear, though, that his interest in abstraction was first aroused while he was working at the Omega Workshop at the very outset of his career. While other Bloomsbury artists, such as Vanessa Bell and Duncan Grant, were essaying abstract easel paintings, he approached it primarily from the angle of practical design, feeling perhaps that what the public would accept on a tray or lampshade or curtain fabric would be altogether too puzzling for them hung on the wall as a self-sufficient work in its own right. All the same, he painted them and kept them, their style changing through the years from the predominantly geometric to the free-form splodges of colour which could almost be called Abstract Expressionist.

All this betokens foreign influence. But at the time he was feeling his way towards a very British fusion. In landscape, which he found increasingly interesting during the later Twenties; and in the portrait, sober observation learnt partly from Cézanne is allied with brilliant colour derived partly from the Fauves and partly, no doubt, from his own Africa-trained eye. The result is, unmistakably, British Post-Impressionism. All his work hangs together very satisfactorily: though he did paint portraits and landscapes and still-lifes and flower paintings, one is never conscious of a generic approach. Basically, he was a painterly painter, and though the subject-matter obviously varied from picture to picture the approach remained remarkably unified.

It was in the early Thirties that he began systematically making portrait drawings, particularly of children, who fascinated him and whose proud parents made this line a useful regular source of income. Sometimes the children's portraits veer over slightly into sentimentality, but in general the ideal, Christopher-Robin child and the quirkish observation of particular character in the individual are kept in happy balance. It is also from this satisfactory period in his life that date his first essays in stage design (unhappily also virtually his last), and his major works of illustration, such as the splendid *Song of Songs* series, which demonstrate to the full his passionate enjoyment of the exotic and his feeling for sheer opulence when the occasion warranted it.

By the mid-Thirties his life and his art took a slightly different turn. Settling in Mexico he encountered a very different terrain, harsh and spiky and russet-tinted, and also, we must presume, a very different kind of painting, that of the extrovert Mexican muralists like Rivera and Orozco, with their dramatic compositions and their disregard for the canons of European good taste. The impact of both of these factors is to be seen in the Mexican paintings, and persists for some time after he had arrived back in Britain. The colour in his paintings of the later Thirties is more muted, the outlines are bolder and rougher: there is some of the monumentality, without the stridency, of the Mexican muralists domesticated into a more familiar framework.

The war years were in every way a break in Wolfe's career, though they did produce some of his most touching portraits, especially of young servicemen, which have some of the fragile awareness of the time that everything was transitory and the youngest and healthiest might not be destined to live much longer. When Wolfe returned to the London art scene after the war, it was at first tentatively, with work in familiar areas like child portrait drawings. But though he sometimes maintained that the war had broken him, a new source of inspiration was at hand. In 1956 he went back to South Africa for nearly three years. The familiar, yet for some thirty-five years unvisited, landscapes of his native land had an unexpected effect on him, muting his colours to gentle harmonies of greens and browns and using the spareness of painterly draughtsmanship he had acquired in Mexico to give a new directness and definition to his pictures of places.

Even this was not quite the end of his stylistic pilgrimage. When he returned again to England, around 1960, he became deeply involved for a while with oriental mysticism, and even painted a few what we might nowadays call psychedelic pictures, visionary scenes showing people shadowed by spirits and surrounded by their psychic auras. This phase did not last long, but perhaps left traces in his final period, when he reverted almost completely to landscape – especially the riverscapes outside the window of his Rotherhithe studio, which are often realized in paint with a glancing fluency, almost sketchiness, which allows in the dazzling light as never before, to illuminate the sky and the water with a brilliance suggestive of Kokoschka and other of the early German Expressionists.

Throughout his career, Wolfe used almost any graphic medium which came to hand. He was adept at painting in oils – his early training at the Slade ensured that – and oils were perhaps the medium in which he showed to most advantage. But he was also a brilliant draughtsman, and a compulsive one: even at the last, given a ball-point or a fibre-tip, he would start sketching portraits of those around or make elaborate designs out of doodles. He was also skilled in that very English medium, watercolour, which he used with a quite un-English force and richness, so that frequently you have to look twice to determine exactly what the medium is.

From his beginnings in practical design for the Omega Workshop he retained, as well as an abiding, if rather shamefaced, interest in abstraction, a fascination with the designer's materials: long after the Omega itself had disbanded he was happy to design and sometimes paint himself humble objects like domestic trays, or turn his hand to industrial design of fabrics and ceramics – the mugs he designed in his eighties for the Royal Academy are among the most successful in the series produced by that august body. And these interests and skills extended themselves to his fine art as well: his illustrations for *The Song of Songs* in particular, with their rich and varied textures, combine collage with drawing and painting to produce something which, somewhere between painting and design, manages to bring out the happiest qualities of both.

There are frequent problems of dating when it comes to Wolfe's drawings, which were mostly done for his own amusement or to keep his hand busy, and unless made in connection with a specific painting were likely to lie around his studio unclassified for years. Also with his abstracts, which, as noted, he did almost throughout his career but kept unshown until 1967. In the illustrations which follow the drawings in particular are arranged according to subject rather than date, though within the subject in roughly chronological order.

42

43

PORTRAIT OF THE ARTIST'S MOTHER
SHE INSISTS HE IS NO BOTHER
HER HAPPY LOOK CONFIRMS THIS TOO
YET I WONDER IF ITS TRUE

44

THE MOTHER OF THIS BIRTHDAY CHILD
NO WONDER SHE LOOKS WAN & WILD
CARE SURROUNDS HER ALL ABOUT
SHE FEARS THE CHAMPAGNE WONT
LAST OUT.

CHAMPAGNE

45

OUR GOLDEN-HAIRED ADONIS NOW
(ITS REALLY GOLD THO SOME SAY TOW)
THE LADIES HOPE HE WONT GROW STOUT
SINCE HIS APPENDIX HAS COME OUT

46

THE YOUTH AND BEAUTY
AT THIS TABLE
MAKES HIS ARTISTIC SOUL
UNSTABLE
IN FRENZIED RAGE HE
TRIES—AND BLUNDERS.
EVEN HIS GENIUS CANT
WORK WONDERS.

47

48

49

50

52

53

54

55

56

57

58

59

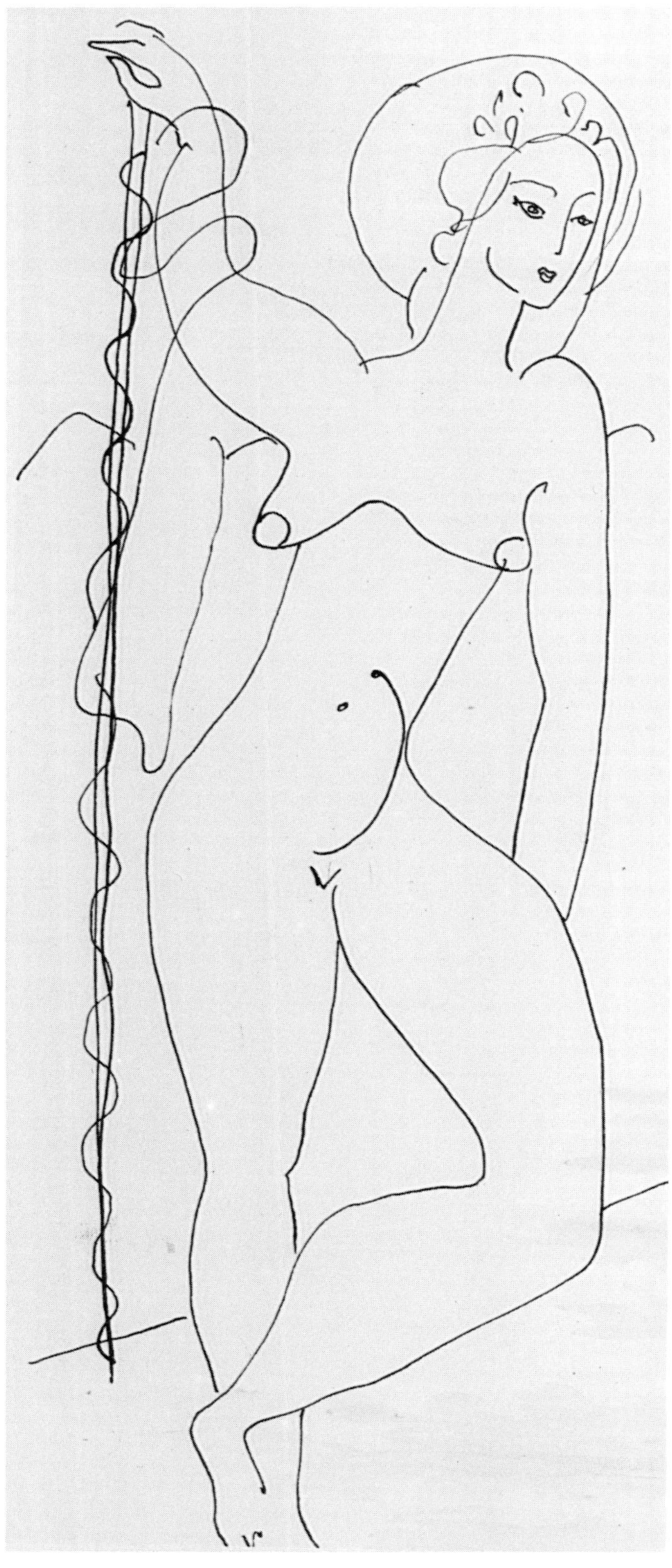

60

61

62

63

64

65

66

67

68

69

70

71

72

73

74

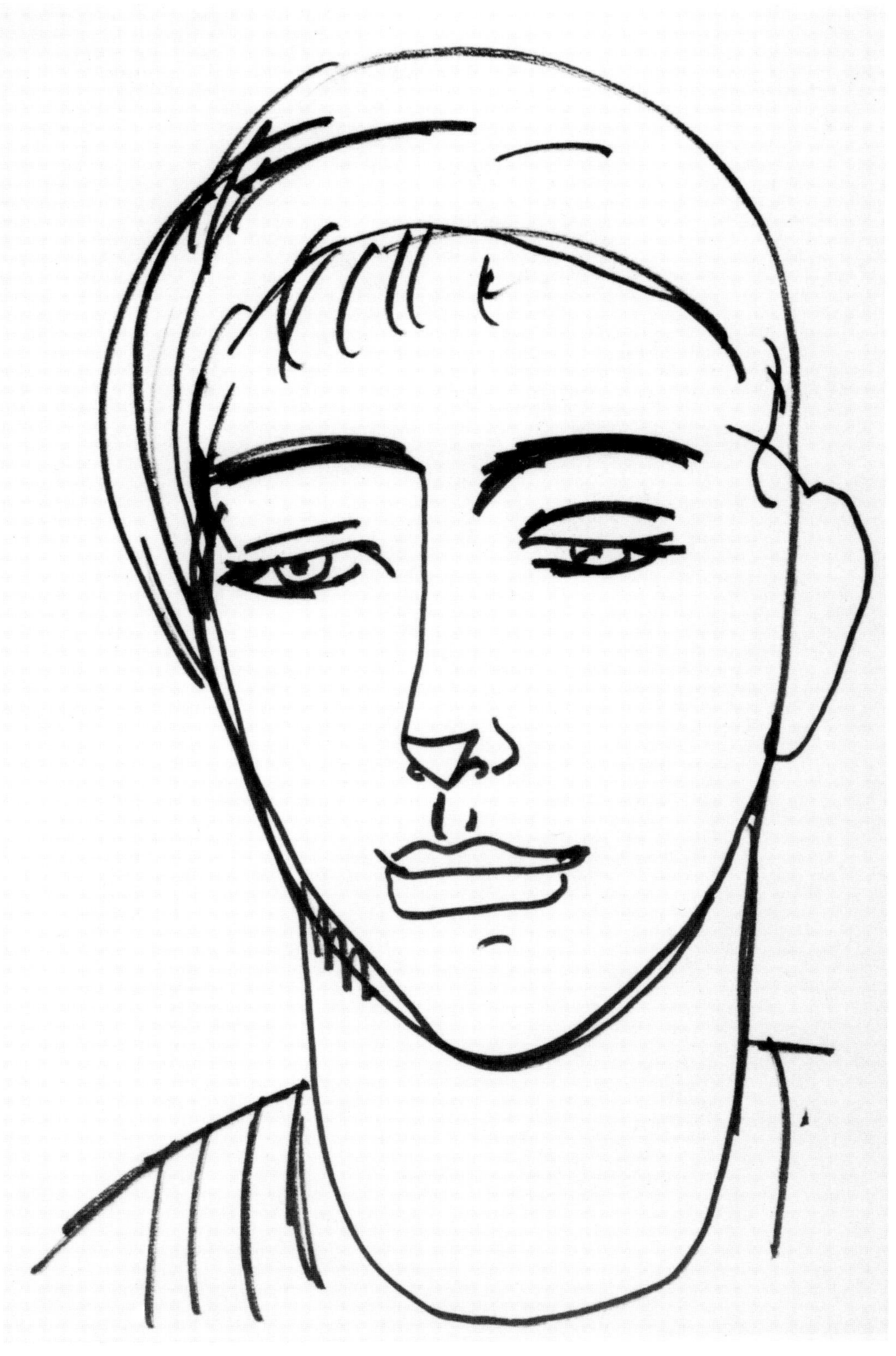

75

76

78

80

81

82

84

86

Wolfe

88

90

91

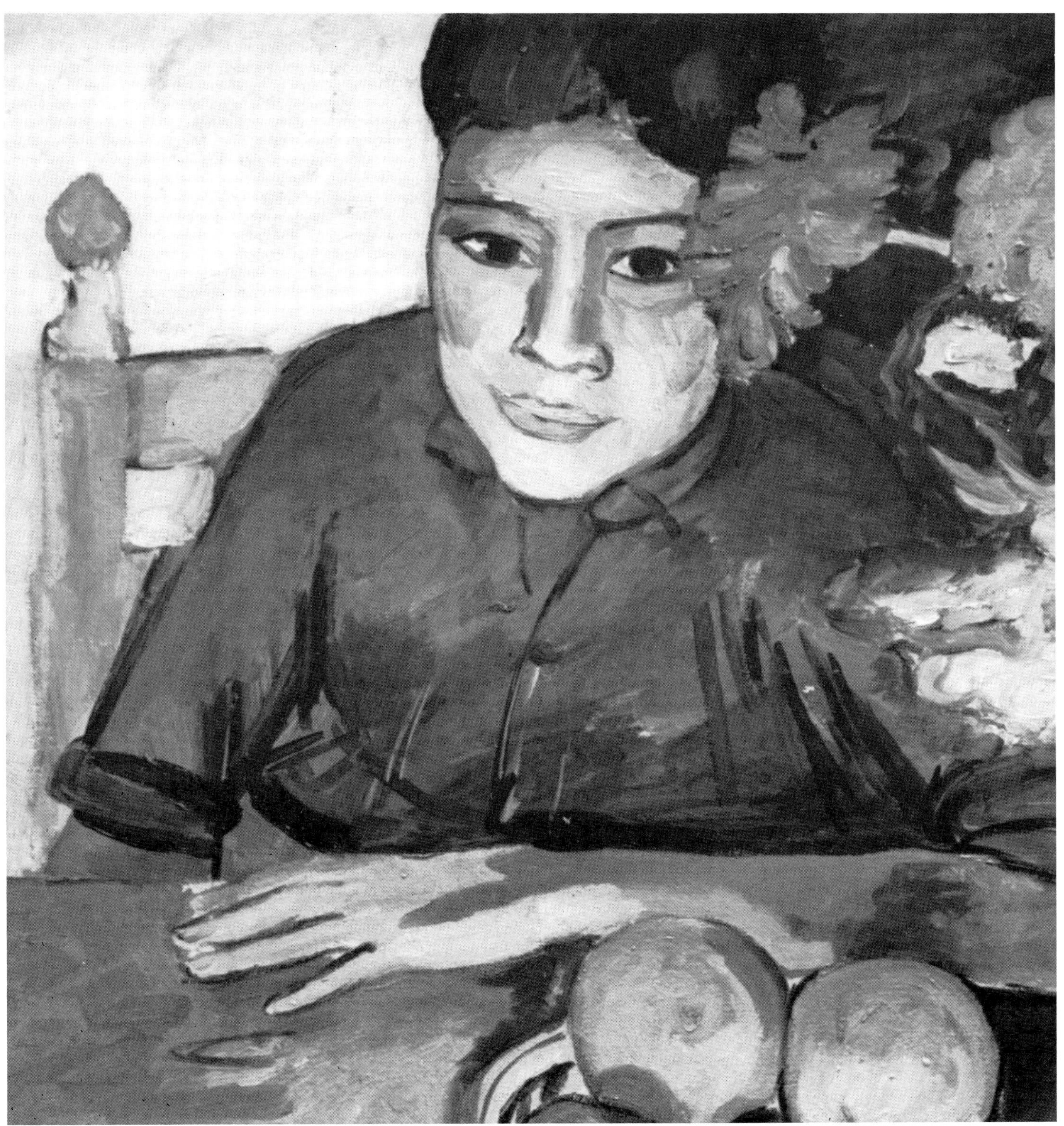

92

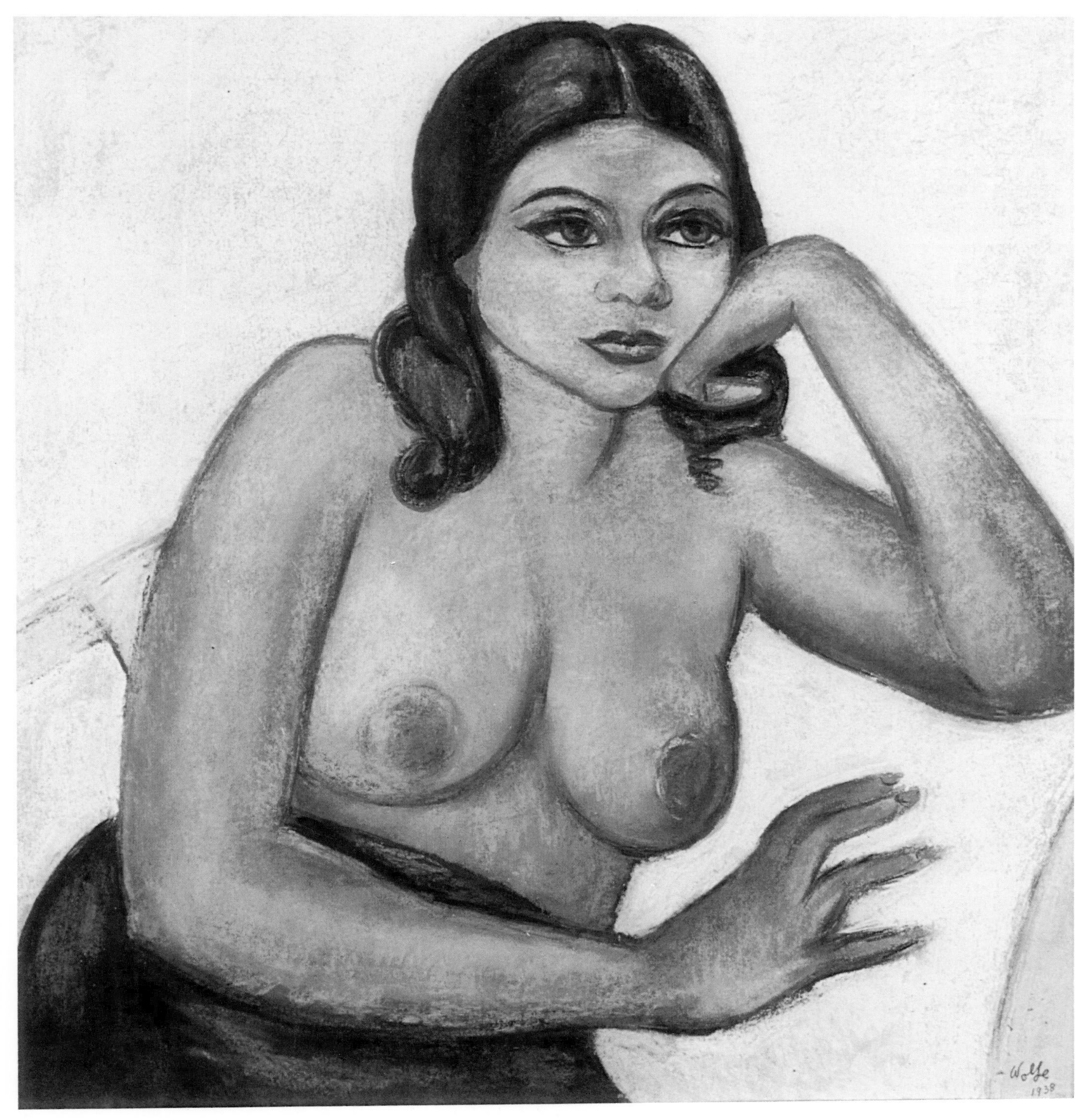


93

94

95

96

98

99

100

101

102

103

104

105

106

107

108

109

110

111

112

113

114

115

116

117

118

119

120

121

122

123

124

126

127

128

130

131

132

133

134

135

136

137

138

139

140

142

143

144

145

146

147

148

149

150

151

152

153

154

156

176

158

159

160

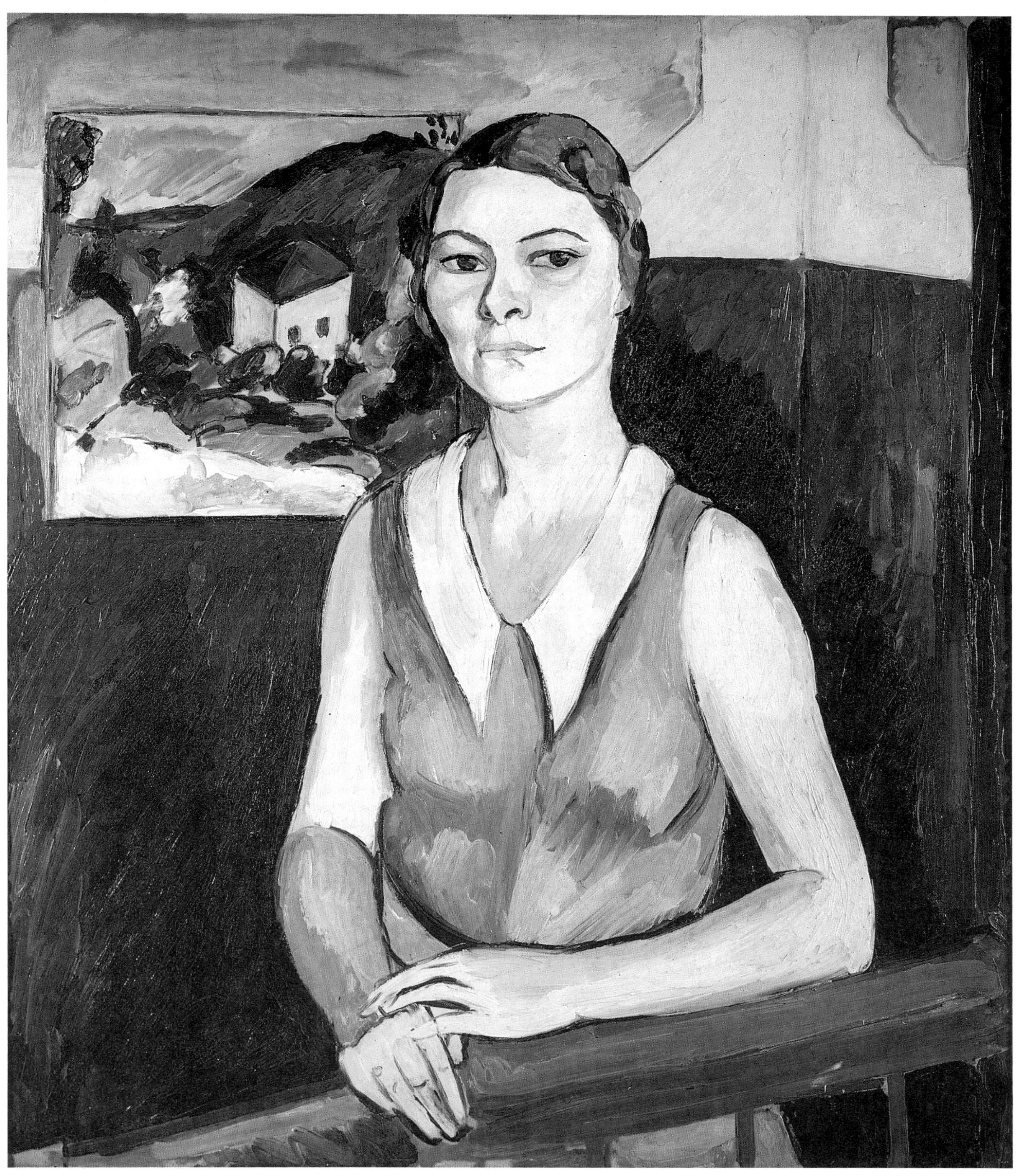

162

164

165

166

167

168

169

170

171

172

there is a kid wot's here in tez,
To him + sez, + sez, + sez—
+ SEZ, "You can't stretch that, my dear,
If you play your backgammon here,
A double six is never treize!"
C.H.T.

174

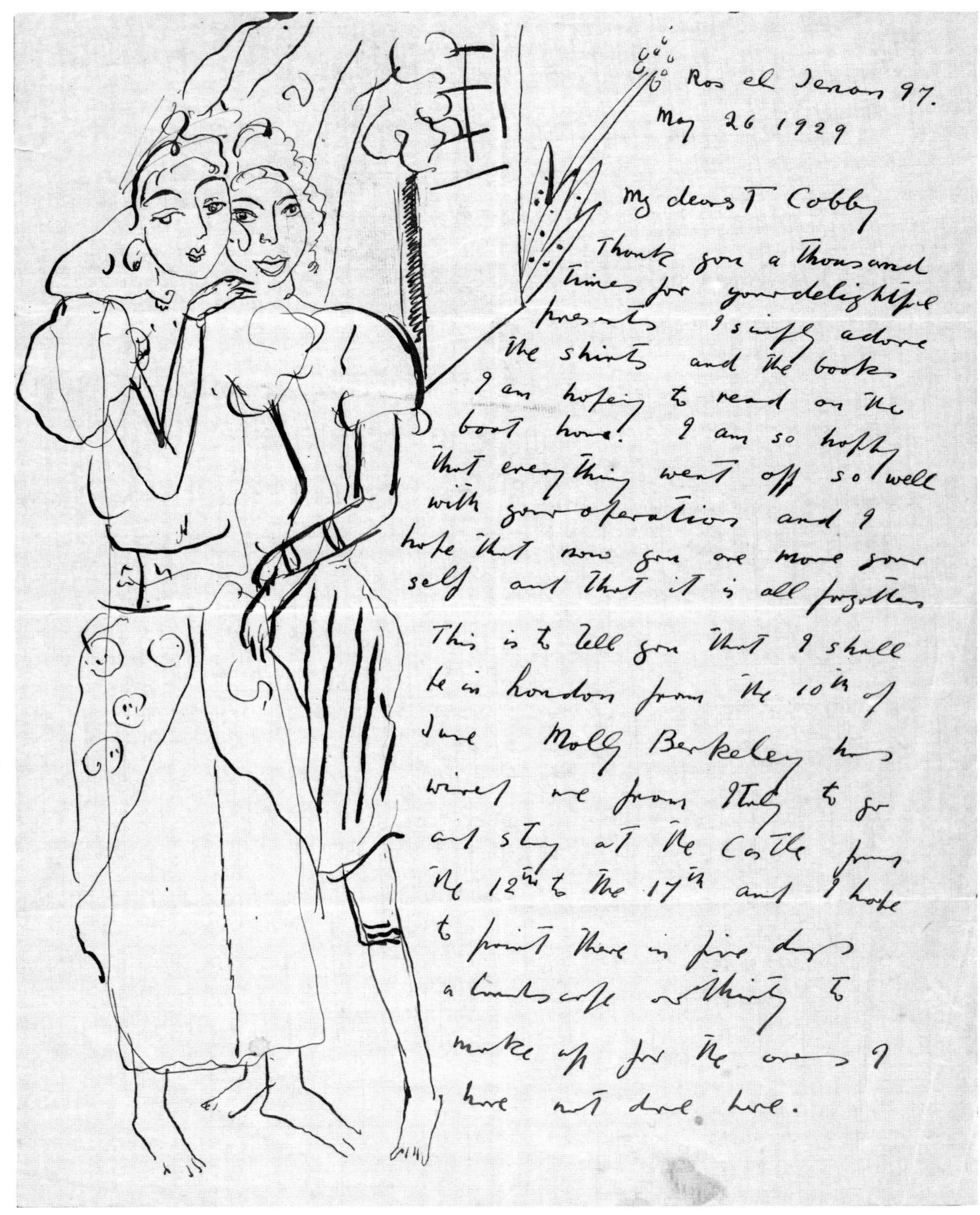

Ras el Jenan 97.
May 26 1929

My dear T Cobby

Thank you a thousand times for your delightful presents I simply adore the shirts and the books I am hoping to read on the boat home. I am so happy that everything went off so well with your operation and I hope that now you are more yourself and that it is all forgotten

This is to tell you that I shall be in London from the 10th of June Molly Berkeley has wired me from Italy to go and stay at the Castle from the 12th to the 17th and I hope to paint there in five days a landscape or thirty to make up for the ones I have not done here.

176

178

179

180

181

182

183

184

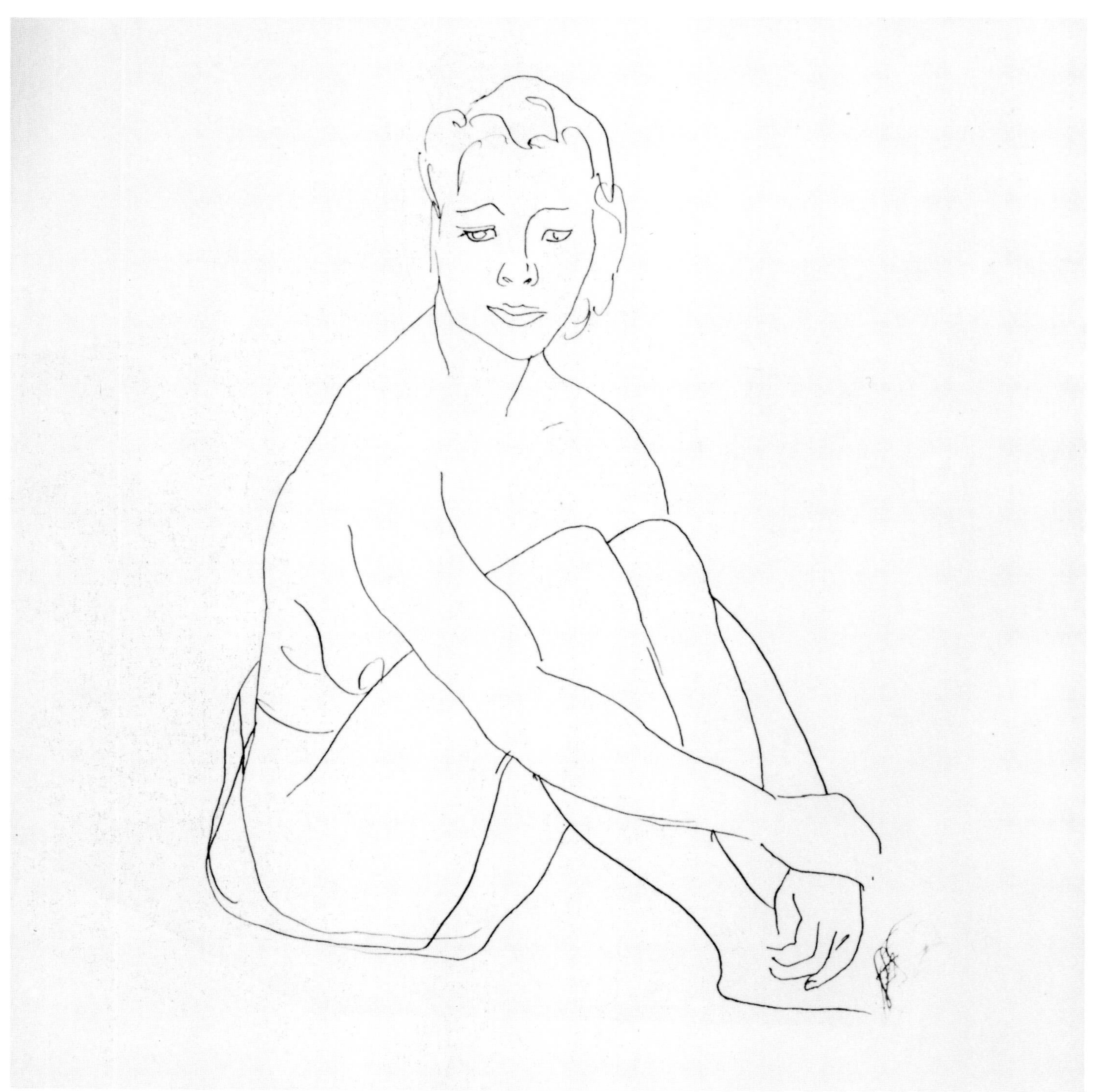

185

186

187

188

189

190

191

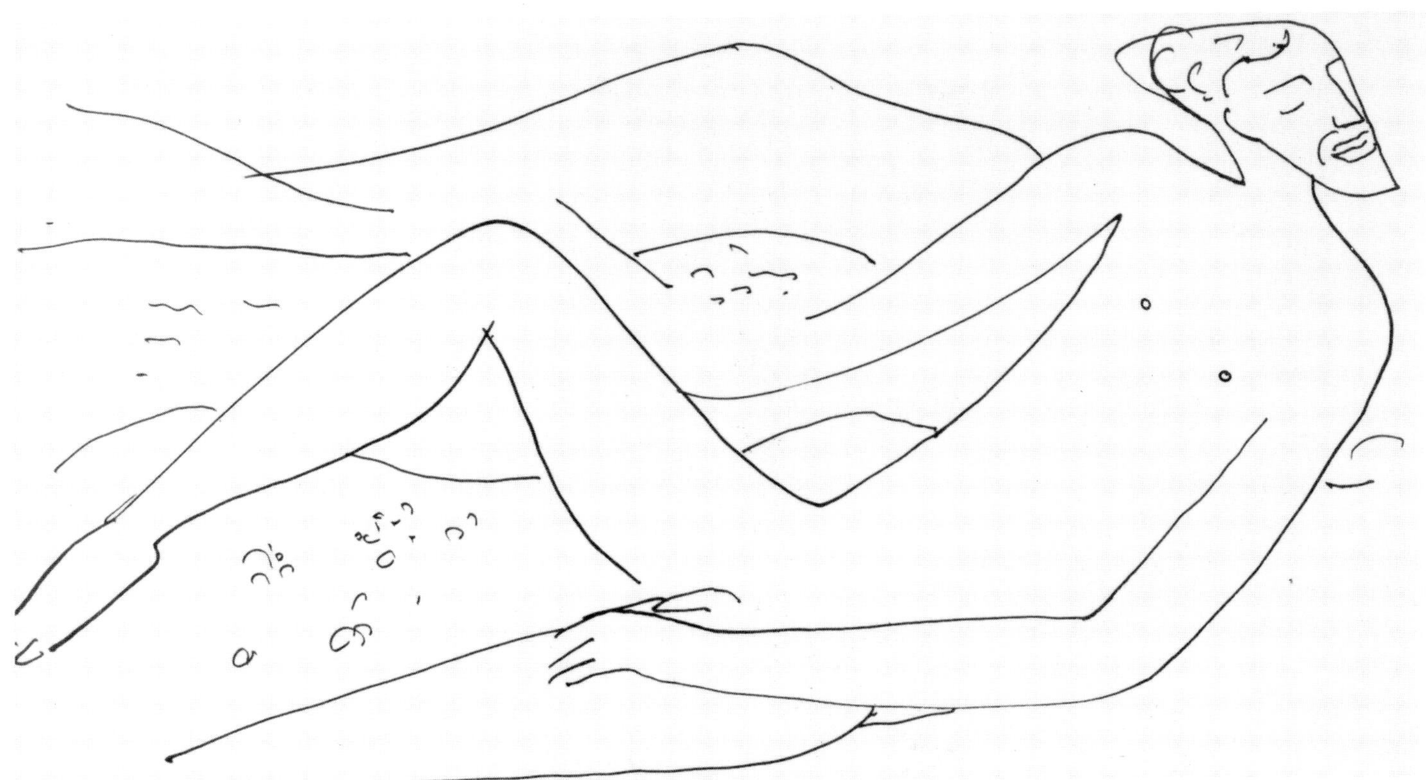

192

Wolff

194

196

197

198

199

200

201

1 Frontispiece: Wolfe in his studio at 77 Bedford Gardens in 1967 with his portrait of Ethel Hayman.

2 Self-portrait.
Exhibited posthumously at the Royal Academy in 1983. Oil. 1920s. 36 x 24.

3 Wolfe in 1918.

4 Portrait of Barclay Donne.
Oil on canvas. 1919. 36 x 24.

5 *Still Life with Omega Cat.*
Oil on canvas. 1918. 10 x 12. Collection: The Charleston Trust.

6 Male nude.
Purple ink. 1918. 12 x 7¾.

7 *Charleston Farm.*
Oil on board. 1918. 9 x 13.

8 *Muse.*
Watercolour. 1918. 15 x 11.

9 Omega Figures.
Watercolour. 1918. 23 x 17.

10 Omega Design.
Pen and watercolour on paper. 1918. 20½ x 26½.

11 Abstract.
Oil on hardboard. 1920s.

12 *Egyptian Journey.*
Ink and watercolour. 1918. 8 x 11¾.

13 *The Matriarch.*
Watercolour. 1918. 10½ x 8.

14 Ruth, the artist's mother.
Brown ink. 1926. 15½ x 11½.

15 South African Miners.
Oil on board. 1920.

16 Florentine model.
Ink. 1923. 12 x 11.

17 *Byba Costa. Florence.*
Oil on canvas. 1923. 23 x 19.

18 *Self portrait.*
Oil on canvas. 1925. 19 x 23½. The 'suicide' self-portrait.

19 *Primavera.*
Ink. 1920s. 7¼ x 5½.

20 *Zhora.*
Oil on canvas. Painted in Fez, 1932.

21 Design for a theatrical backdrop.
Ink. 1931. 8 x 10½.

22 Set for James Laver's play *The Heart was not burned.* 1938.

23 Study for the *Song of Songs.*
Ink on silver paper. 1930. 18¾ x 14¾.

24 *Song of Songs.*
Lithograph on silver paper. Designed 1930, editioned 1980. Edition 250. 14 x 10½.

25 *Song of Songs.*
Lithograph on silver paper. Edition 250. 14 x 10½.

26 *Two Mexican boys.*
Pastel. 1935. 31½ x 23¼.

27 *Mexican landscape.*
Oil. 1935. 16 x 12½.

28 *Mexican flower piece.*
Oil on board. 1936. 34½ x 22½.

29 *Laugharne Castle.*
Oil on canvas. 1937. 31 x 44½. Trustees of the Tate Gallery.

30 Wolfe in about 1940.

31 Jet Fairley seated in studio.
Ink. 1930. 20 x 13½.

32 *Portmeirion, North Wales.*
Oil on canvas. 1946.

33 Male nude – Ischian fisherman.
Pencil. 1946. 16¾ x 13½.

34 *Ischian sailor.*
Oil. 1946. 23½ x 19½.

35 *Kenilworth. Capetown.*
Oil on canvas. 1957. 30 x 43.

36 *The Harbour, Ischia.*
Oil. 1946.

37 *The Harbour, Ischia.*
Oil. 1946. Painted from almost exactly the same viewpoint as 36, but on a stormy day.

38 *Still-life.*
Painted in South Africa. Oil on canvas. 1956-8.

39 *Tower Bridge from Rotherhithe.*
1958-60.

40 Wolfe's studio in Rotherhithe.

41 Wolfe at his studio in Rotherhithe in the late 1970s.

42 Wolfe painting in his studio.

43, 44, 45, 46 Cartoons with verses.
From a series done mostly in Tangiers. *c.* 1930.

47 *Modi's Model.*
Pencil. 1926. 18 x 13.

48 Woman washing.
Pencil. 1918. 13½ x 10.

49 Seated Woman.
Ink. 1918. 13 x 9.

50 Seated woman.
Ink. 1920. 13 x 9.

51 Male nude.
Pencil. 1920. 16½ x 11.

52 *Young man in a blue shirt.*
Oil on canvas. 1928. 33½ x 23.

53 *The Reader.*
Oil on canvas. 35 x 61.

54 Moroccan girl.
Ink. *c.* 1930. 10½ x 8.

55 *Flora.*
Ink. 1930s. 10½ x 7¾.

56 Man with a beard.
Ink. 10 x 7½.

57 *Lovers.*
Ink. 9 x 12.

58 Figures on a beach.
Ink. 7½ x 13.

59 Nude woman with a staff.
Ink. 10½ x 4½.

60 Reclining female nude.
Pencil. 1940s.

61 Standing female nude.
Ink and watercolour. 12 x 13.

62 Back view of reclining female nude.
Ink. 8 x 10.

63 Reclining nude, Jet.
Ink. 1930. 14 x 10.

64 Reclining nude.
Pencil. 1940s. 14¾ x 23¼.

65 *Portrait of Diana Dent.*
Oil on canvas. 1924. 28½ x 47½.

66 Madonna.
Ink. 8 x 6½.

67 Two women.
Blue and black watercolour. 26½ x 19½.

68 *Mothers and Children.*
Gouache. 1918. 12 x 10.

69 *Mexican woman.*
Oil on board. 26 x 20.

70 *Mother and Child.*
Pastel. 1930.

71 *Portrait of Mrs Fairley (Jet).*
Oil on canvas.

72 Child.
Ink on silver paper. 19½ x 13½.

73 Head of a woman.
Ink. 14½ x 10½.

74 Head.
Ink on grey paper. 19 x 12½.

75 Young girl.
Ink. Late 1930s. 18 x 15.

76 Angel.
Ink. 11 x 8½.

77 *Woman in Interior, Tangiers.*
Oil on canvas. 1930.

78 *The Doorway.* Tangiers.
Oil on canvas. 1930. Patterson Collection, Belfast Museum and Art Gallery.

79 *Aisha of the Kasha.*
Oil on canvas. 20½ x 16½.

80 *Moroccan flower-piece.*
Oil on canvas. *c.*1930.

81 Head of Mina, Tangiers.
Ink. 1930. 17¾ x 13¾.

82 Arab, Tangiers.
Crayon. 1930. 13 x 10.

83 *Tangiers.*
Oil. 1931.

84 *Arabs, Morocco.*
Oil on canvas. 1930.

85 *Portrait of Zhora.*
Oil on canvas. 1930. 25½ x 21.

86 *'Cardiff' Mohammed Ben Laitz.*
Painted Tangiers 1930. Oil on board. 33 x 24.
Bootle Museum and Art Gallery.

87 Female nude, drawing for oil.
Morocco, 1930.

88 *North African Dream.*
Pastel. 1930. 39 x 27¾.

89 *Mexican Woman.*
Pastel. 1936. 30 x 24.

90 *Mexican Lovers.*
Ink. 1935. 10 x 7.

91 *Mexican Boy.*
Oil on canvas. 1935.

92 Detail of 91.

93 *Veruna.*
Pastel. Mexico 1935.

94 Reclining female nude.
Pastel.

95 The Harbour, Tangiers.
Oil. 1954. This and the following paintings indicate Wolfe's passion for serial painting, dealing with the same subject from slightly different viewpoints, in different formats, in different weathers.

96 The Harbour, Tangiers
Oil, 1954.

97 The Harbour, Tangiers.
Oil. 1954.

98 *Ischia.*
Oil on canvas. 1947.

99 *Windy day, Tangiers.*
Oil on canvas. 1932. 20½ x 25.

100 *Ardmore, Waterford* (Ireland).
Oil on canvas. 1937. 19 x 24.

101 *North Wales landscape with Snowdon in the distance.*
Oil on canvas. 1945. 20 x 24.

102 *Penrhyndendraeth, North Wales.*
Oil on canvas. 1947.

103 *Tolleneaux.*
Oil on canvas. 1950s.

104 *Marbella.*
Oil on canvas. 1950s.

105 *Ghajn Tuta, Gozo.*
Oil on canvas. 1950s.

106 *San Roquet.*
Oil on canvas. 1933. 30 x 39.

107 *Portrait of a woman.*

108 *Mediterranean Landscape.*
Oil on canvas.

109 Exterior of Spanish church. Charcoal drawing.
1950. 16½ x 12.

110 Interior of Spanish church. Charcoal drawing.
1955. 19½ x 12¾.

111 *Ischia.*
Oil on canvas. 1947.

112 *Stuben's Farm.*
Oil on canvas. 1955. 25 x 30.

113 *The Tresfon Farm, Cape Province, South Africa.*
Oil on canvas. 1956.

114 *The Tresfon Farm, Cape Province, South Africa.*
Oil on canvas. 1956.

115 *Still Life with Head.*
Oil on canvas. 1920s. 24½ x 30.

116 *Still Life with Newspaper.*
Oil on canvas. 1929. 30 x 25.

117 *Flowerpiece.*
Oil on canvas. 1949.

118 *The Green Lilies.*
Oil on canvas. Painted in South Africa. 1956.

119 *Dahlias on Backgammon Board.*
Oil on canvas. 1946.

120 *Still Life with Clock.*
Oil on canvas. 1954.

121 *Still Life.* South Africa.
Oil on canvas. 1956.

122 *Landscape, South Africa.*
Oil on canvas. 1950. A variant of this picture is seen in the background of 121.

123 *Flowerpiece.* Oil on canvas. Late 1950s.

124 *Flowerpiece with a Bowl of Fruit.*
Oil on canvas. 1945. 39 x 29.

125 *Plant in the Window.*
Oil on canvas. 30 x 19.

126 *Flowers in a Glass Vase.*
Oil on canvas. 16 x 10. Courtesy of the Belgrave Gallery, London.

127 Abstract.
Oil on board.

128 *Still Life with Oriental Carpet.*
Oil on canvas. 1920s.

129 *Still Life for Adeline.*
Oil on canvas. 1930s.

130 *Still Life.*
Oil on canvas. Variant on 129.

131 *Mexican Still Life.*
1935. Oil on canvas.

132 *Sleeping Child.*
Ink and watercolour. Early 1950s.

133 *Lady Isobel Child Villiers,* daughter of the Earl of Jersey.
Watercolour. 1953.

134 *The Son of Robert Adeane.*
Watercolour. 1954.

135 *Portrait of a Boy.*
Oil on canvas.

136 *Archie Hamilton,* son of Lord Hamilton of Dalziell.
Pencil drawing. Early 1950s.

137, 138 Two studies of the same boy sitter.
1956. 17 x 13½.

139 Boy. Pencil drawing. 1950s. 20½ x 13½.

140 Boy in blue. Watercolour. 1950. 17½ x 11½.

141 Boy. Ink drawing. 1950s.

142 *Portrait of Ivan.*
Oil on canvas. 1958.

143 *David Cleghorne Thompson.*
Oil on canvas. 25 x 19.

144 *Portrait of Arnold Bennett.*
Oil on canvas. 1918. 43 x 31.

145 Portrait drawing of a man.
Charcoal. 1920s.

146 *J. Yeargoode.*
Oil on canvas. 1950.

147 Man smoking.
Ink on silver board. 1930. 21 x 14½.

148 *Self-portrait.*
Ink. 1930. 14 x 10.

149 Portrait of a young man.
Pastel. 1920s.

150 Portrait and sitter.

151 Head of a young man.
Watercolour, yellow and green. 1950. 28 x 16.

152 Head of a young man.
Oil on canvas. The background would seem to be the harbour at Tangiers (*see* plates 95-97).

153 Head of woman.
Charcoal drawing.

154 Head of woman.
Oil on canvas. 1930s.

155 Portrait of a girl.
Oil on canvas. 1950s.

156 Portrait of Gypsy Lang.
Oil on canvas. 1926.

157 Portrait of a woman.
Oil on canvas. 1950s.

158 Portrait of a woman.
Oil on canvas. 1940s.

159 *Girl with Sunflowers.*
Oil on canvas. 1920s.

160 *The Yellow Hat* (Mrs Geoffrey Garratt).
Probably painted at Tangiers. Oil on board. 1933.
31¾ x 25½.

161 *Portrait of Mrs Henderson.*
Oil on board. 1940s.

162 *Portrait, Tangiers.*
Oil on canvas. 1930/31.

163 Woman with her hair up.
Ink drawing. 1940s. 11 x 8.

164 *Mrs Jefferson.*
Pastel. 1946. 33½ x 25½.

165 *Elise Otley.*
Blue pencil. 1940. 15½ x 18¾.

166 Head of a woman.
Charcoal drawing.

167 *Suzy Burgess.*
Lithograph. 1958. 22¼ x 17¼.

168 Head of a woman.
Ink drawing. 1950s. 10½ x 8.

169 *'Queen'.*
1950. 9 x 6.

170 *Head at the sea.*
11 x 8.

171 *Portrait of Nancy Feaver.*
Oil on canvas. 1966.

172 Frontispiece to *The Dancing Beggars,* a book of poems by John Garratt.
1946. Reproduced actual size.

173 Illustrated letter to 'Cobby'.

174 Illustrated letter.

175 Scottish piper.
Ink drawing. 13 x 10.

176 *Private Tim Hamilton.*
Pastel. 1940.

177 *P.C. 77.*
Oil on canvas. 43¾ x 30¾. Trustees of the Tate Gallery.

178 *Dutch Sailor.*
Oil on canvas. 1940s. 32 x 24½.

179 *Pat Nelson.*
Oil on canvas. 1930. 31½ x 26¾.

180 *Pat Nelson.*
Oil on canvas. 1930.

181 Nude black model.
Rotherhithe. 1950s. 17¾ x 14.

182 Nude black model in armchair.
Ink on burnt orange paper. 18 x 14½.

183 Female nude on sofa.
Ink. 19¾ x 12½.

184 Seated nude.
Charcoal. 1950. 25 x 18¾.

185 Seated nude.
Ink on grey paper. 12 x 13.

186 Woman in a dressing gown.
Ink and wash. 13½ x 10.

187 *Liza Beer.*
Oil on canvas.

188 *Catherine, Rotherhithe.*
Oil on canvas. 1955. 26 x 32.

189 *Catherine, nude.*
Watercolour. 1950s. 17½ x 21¾.

190 Nude.
Blue pencil. 1950. 17½ x 23½.

191 Nude, Rotherhithe.
Ink on lilac paper. 1950. 11½ x 16½.

192 Reclining male nude.
Ink. 1950s. 5 x 8.

193 Seated nude.
Fibre-pen. 1960s.

194 Young girl.
Fibre-pen. 1960s. 11 x 8.

195 *In the cafe.*
Fibre-pen. 1960s. 12¼ x 9¾.

196 *Landscape, South Africa.*
Oil on canvas. 1956. 10½ x 14½.

197 *Rotherhithe.*
Oil on canvas. 1958.

198 *River scene.*
Late 1950s. Oil on canvas.

199 *Tower Bridge.*
Late 1950s. 8¾ x 16¾.

200 *The Pool of London.*
Drawing. 1950s.

201 *Landscape, South Africa.*
Oil on canvas. 1956.

## Edward Wolfe: Principal Exhibitions

***One-man Shows:***

1919 At Maynard Keynes's home, 46 Gordon Square, London
1920 Leon Levson Gallery, Johannesburg
1926 Mayor Gallery, London
1929 Warren Gallery, London
1930 London Artists' Association
1936 Lefevre Gallery, London
1938 Mayor Gallery, London
1944 Redfern Gallery, London
1946 Florida Gallery, Naples
1948 Lefevre Gallery, London
1950 Touring show in Salford, Cardiff and Liverpool
1951 Mayor Gallery, London (watercolours and drawings)
1953 Galerie de Seine, Paris
O'Hana Gallery, London
1954 Mayor Gallery, London (portraits of children)
1956 Gainsborough Gallery, Johannesburg; also in Cape Town, Stellenbosch, Port Elizabeth
1967 Arts Council retrospective: London, Norwich, Wolverhampton, Derby
1973 Mayor Gallery, London
1977 Artists' Market, London (Pictures of the Thames)
1979 Fieldbourne Gallery, London (Sixty Years of Painting)
1980 Patrick Seale Gallery, London
1983 Patrick Seale Gallery, London (Early Decorative Art – Bloomsbury Period)
1986 Alpine Gallery, London (with Duncan Grant)
Odette Gilbert Gallery, London

***Selected Group Shows***

1918 Omega Workshop
London Group, Eighth Exhibition, Mansard Gallery, London
1922 London Group, Sixteenth Exhibition, Mansard Gallery, London
1923 London Group, Eighteenth Exhibition, Mansard Gallery, London
London Group, Nineteenth Exhibition, Mansard Gallery, London
Venice Biennale
1925 London Group, Twenty-second Exhibition, R.W.S. Galleries, London
1926 Seven and Five, Beaux Arts Gallery, London
1927 Seven and Five, Beaux Arts Gallery, London
1928 Seven and Five, Beaux Arts Gallery, London
1934 London Artists' Association, Cooling Gallery, London
1943 London Group, Victoria Art Gallery, Bath
1944 American Art Centre, New York
1948 Bristol City Art Gallery
1951 London Group, New Burlington Galleries, London
1964 Royal Academy Summer Exhibition (yearly until 1982)